D0977025

Early praise for *The 5 Elements of Effective Thinking*

"*The 5 Elements* is an enormously insightful examination of what constitutes effective thinking. Everyone will find something of value in it."
—**Morton O. Schapiro, president of Northwestern University**

"I highly recommend this book for instructors who care more about their students than test scores, for students who care more about learning than their GPA, for leaders of society and masters of the universe who care more about serving the public good than increasing their profit margin, and for artists who constantly remind us of the human condition. *The 5 Elements of Effective Thinking* provides comfort in a world that has lost its equilibrium."
—**Christopher J. Campisano, director of Princeton University's Program in Teacher Preparation**

"Edward Burger and Michael Starbird became renowned scholars and educators by demonstrating that mathematical expertise is within the reach of the general population and not confined to those with the 'right' aptitude. With the publication of this remarkably wise and useful book, they extend their pedagogical principles to the general realm of practical affairs and the entire range of academic endeavor. Regardless of the reader's background, *The 5 Elements* offers highly applicable and original lessons on how to think."
—**John W. Chandler, president emeritus of Hamilton College and Williams College**

"So this is how Newton stood on the shoulders of giants! Burger and Starbird outline the basic methods of genius—so that ordinary people, too, can see further than others."
—**Robert W. Kustra, president of Boise State University**

"I spectacularly love this book. It made the greatest impact on me a book possibly could because I hold these ideas in such high regard and they landed in my hands at the perfect time. My overarching response to *The 5 Elements of Effective Thinking* is pure delight, great appreciation, and confidence in myself and in what lies ahead."
—**Kyle C., undergraduate mathematics major**

"This book took me on an emotional rollercoaster, made clear some biases I have toward myself, and helped me to see the world in a new way."

—**Elle V., undergraduate biology major**

"There are a lot of great things about this book. It is filled with many wonderful quotes, witty humor, fun exercises, historical and personal examples, and stuff that really gets you thinking. I also found myself quietly laughing out loud in the library several times. I have already recommended this book to people who want to take a different approach to thinking. I was very fortunate, and sometimes I think, destined, to receive this book on the first day of college."

—**Luis H., undergraduate history major**

"While reading *The 5 Elements*, I learned more about how I should think, study, and understand than during any other experience in my life. Every chapter resonated so well with me that I am already changing the way I go through my classes, homework, and life."

—**Nirav S., undergraduate mechanical engineering major**

"This book is captivating because it changes the average thoughts of learning by teaching new ones and highlighting them through examples of current students and historic geniuses. The book shows that geniuses are average people with different ways of thinking and learning. I found this new insight inspiring."

—**Lauren L., undergraduate psychology major**

"When I picked up this book to read for a class, I was dreading it. After the first few pages, I couldn't put it down. I've always had an idea of what I've needed to do in order to become a better student, but this material was laid out in a way that was not only inspirational, but fun to read. The basics of learning, understanding, and creating are all within this text."

—**Scott G., undergraduate civil engineering major**

The 5 Elements of Effective Thinking

The 5 Elements of Effective Thinking

Edward B. Burger and Michael Starbird

PRINCETON UNIVERSITY PRESS

PRINCETON AND OXFORD

Library of Congress Cataloging-in-Publication Data

Burger, Edward B., 1963–

        The 5 elements of effective thinking / Edward B. Burger and Michael
    Starbird.

            p. cm.

        ISBN 978-0-691-15666-8 (hardcover : alk. paper) 1. Thought and
    thinking. I. Starbird, Michael P. II. Title. III. Title: Five elements of effec-
    tive thinking.

        BF441.B9247 2012

        153.4'2—dc23   2012014372

British Library Cataloging-in-Publication Data is available

This book has been composed in AppleSymbols, Baskerville 10 Pro,
    John Sans Heavy Pro, John Sans Text Pro

Printed on acid-free paper. ∞

Printed in the United States of America

10 9 8

Contents

Preface
Thinking Makes the Difference   vii

Introduction
Elements of Effective Thinking, Learning,
   and Creating   1

 Earth

1. Grounding Your Thinking   13
   UNDERSTAND DEEPLY

   Understand simple things deeply   15
   Clear the clutter—seek the essential   26
   See what's there   31
   See what's missing   41
   Final thoughts: Deeper is better   44

 Fire

2. Igniting Insights through Mistakes   47
   FAIL TO SUCCEED

   *Welcome accidental missteps—let your errors be
      your guide*   51
   Finding the right question to the wrong answer   64
   Failing by intent   66
   Final thoughts: A modified mind-set   71

Air

3. Creating Questions out of Thin Air   73
BE YOUR OWN SOCRATES

How answers can lead to questions   75
Creating questions enlivens your curiosity   82
What's the real *question?*   86
*Final thoughts: The art of creating questions and
        active listening*   93

 Water

4. Seeing the Flow of Ideas   95
LOOK BACK, LOOK FORWARD

Understanding current ideas through the flow of ideas   98
Creating new ideas from old ones   106
Final thoughts: "Under construction" is the norm   117

 **The Quintessential Element**

5. Engaging Change   119
TRANSFORM YOURSELF

 Summary

A Way to Provoke Effective Thinking   136
A Brief Review

Share Your Own Stories of Effective Thinking   149
Acknowledgments   151
About the Authors   155

Preface
Thinking Makes the Difference

I think, therefore I am.

—René Descartes

The root of success in everything, from academics to business to leadership to personal relationships and everything else, is thinking—whether it's thinking disguised as intuition or as good values or as decision making or problem solving or creativity, it's all thinking.

So it is not a surprise that thinking more effectively is the key to success for students, professionals, business leaders, artists, writers, politicians, and all of us living our everyday lives. Doing anything better requires *effective thinking*—that is, coming up with more imaginative ideas, facing complicated problems, finding new ways to solve them, becoming aware of hidden possibilities, and then taking action.

What *is* a surprise is that the basic methods for thinking more clearly, more innovatively, more effectively are fundamentally the same in all areas of life—in school, in business, in the arts, in personal life, in sports, in everything. The other surprise is that those methods of effective thinking can be described, taught, and learned. They are not inborn gifts of a special few. They are not so esoteric that only geniuses can master them. All of us can learn them and use them, and that is what this book is about.

We, the authors, did not begin our careers with the goal of discovering strategies of effective thinking. We began our careers teaching the abstract ideas of mathematics. But over the years we came to realize that what actually makes a difference are a few habits of thinking that people can apply in everyday life—methods that are not mathematical at all. This book offers thought-provoking ways to provoke thought. These strategies have inspired many people in all walks of life to become more successful, and we hope that you too will create success through effective thinking.

Introduction
Elements of Effective Thinking, Learning, and Creating

> **I know quite certainly that I myself have no special talent.**
> **Curiosity, obsession and dogged endurance, combined**
> **with self-criticism, have brought me to my ideas.**
>
> **—Albert Einstein**

A wondrously romantic belief is that brilliant students are born brilliant and brilliant thinkers magically produce brilliant ideas: *A+*, the star student aces the exam; *click*, Edison invents the lightbulb; *liftoff*, the Wright brothers soar into the sky; *abracadabra*, J. K. Rowling apparates Harry Potter; *yea*, the Founding Fathers resolve the Bill of Rights; *whoosh*, Ralph Lauren turns heads on fashion's runways; *eureka*, Einstein teases his hair and relativity falls out. We can all marvel at these fanciful visions of leaps of genius, but we should not be fooled into believing that they're reality. Brilliant students and brilliant innovators create their own victories by practicing habits of thinking that inevitably carry them step-by-step to works of greatness. No leaps are involved—a few basic strategies of thought can lead to effective learning, understanding, and innovation. More importantly, *you* yourself can master and apply those strategies. This book presents practical, proven methods of effective thinking and creativity that lead to inevitable success in life.

We, the authors, are teachers. We have taught hundreds of thousands of students and adults how to think more effectively. Countless times we have encountered individuals with potential and watched the drama of life's transformation unfold—or not. Anne and Adam struggle with ideas, understand the basics, learn from mistakes, ask questions—and thrive. Fiona and Frank, with the same native talent, start at the same place, but they memorize without understanding, fear error, avoid uncertainty—and do not succeed. This book is about what makes the difference.

Education does not stop with the end of your formal schooling. Even if your formal school days are long past, you are still a student and, hopefully, will always be one. You can choose to learn habits of thought that will help you to meet the ongoing challenges of life—personal, professional, and societal.

Imagine Marie Curie, Albert Einstein, and William Shakespeare as students. Today we know them as famous geniuses, but when they were in school, they didn't walk around wearing a "future genius" button. Instead, they just looked at the world differently by applying habits of mind that allowed them to discover and create new and profound ideas. While we can celebrate famous geniuses and be inspired by their remarkable stories, this book is about *you*—a real person with strengths and weaknesses—not a mythologized hero. Look down at your shirt—if you don't see a "FUTURE GENIUS" button, then you too have the potential to innovate. Creativity is not a matter of magical inspiration. This book describes habits that will automatically cause *you* to regularly produce new knowledge and insight. Remember: Extraordinary people are just ordinary people who are thinking differently—and that could be you.

Ordinary students can attain extraordinary heights. Mark was one of our mathematics students whose work at the beginning of the semester was truly dismal. He was so lost that his homework assignments were neither right nor wrong—they were simply nonsense. He merely recycled math terms that he wrote down during class discussions without even knowing their meaning. It was as if he were writing a poem in a language that he himself did not understand. Although he was genuinely dedicated, Mark appeared to be the textbook example of a *lost cause*.

By the end of the semester, however, Mark had transformed himself into a different person—a person who was able to think about mathematics in clever and imaginative ways. As the term came to a close, he devised a creative and correct solution to a difficult, long-standing challenge that no one else in the class was able to resolve. At some point during the semester, Mark had the epiphany that mathematics had meaning and that he could make sense of it. He returned to the most basic ideas of the subject—ideas that he had seen years before but never truly grasped. He floundered when he viewed learning as memorizing techniques and repeating words. He succeeded when he sought to understand fundamental ideas deeply. With his new mind-set, building up a solid understanding of the subject was relatively easy, and his success in the class was inevitable.

The principles of understanding the unknown and finding creative insights that transformed Mark's life can be taught, learned, and applied broadly across disciplines and professions. We have seen these methods of thinking transform otherwise ordinary people into innovative leaders, authors, artists, financial gurus, teachers, film producers, scientists, and, in a number of cases, multimillionaires.

Education is what survives when what has been learned has been forgotten.
   —B. F. Skinner

Given that we, the authors, are professors, it is not surprising that many stories in this book take place in classroom settings. However, we have also taught tens of thousands of lifelong learners. So when we offer illustrations from our school experiences, we hope that you will view them literally if you are in the classroom (as either a student or a teacher), or metaphorically if you now find yourself outside the ivy-covered walls of the academy. When Aesop wrote "The Tortoise and the Hare," he was not aiming exclusively at the turtle market. Throughout life we frequently face challenges analogous to taking tests, earning grades, and understanding course material. Instead of taking formal tests, we encounter daunting questions from employers or even family and friends; instead of earning grades, we are judged in the workplace and in social settings; instead of understanding course material, we regularly need to master new skills and absorb new knowledge to keep up with a rapidly changing world. All our stories have direct relevance to you and your life.

Five elements of thinking and learning

The surprising fact is that just a few learnable strategies of thinking can make you more effective in the classroom, the boardroom, and the living room. You can personally *choose* to become more successful by adopting five learnable habits, which, in this book, we not only explain in detail but also make concrete and practical. Here in this section we briefly introduce those important habits to come.

Understand deeply:

Don't face complex issues head-on; first understand simple ideas deeply. Clear the clutter and expose what is really important. Be brutally honest about what you know and don't know. Then see what's missing, identify the gaps, and fill them in. Let go of bias, prejudice, and preconceived notions. There are degrees to understanding (it's not just a yes-or-no proposition) and you can always heighten yours. Rock-solid understanding is the foundation for success.

Make mistakes:

Fail to succeed. Intentionally get it wrong to inevitably get it even more right. Mistakes are great teachers— they highlight unforeseen opportunities and holes in your understanding. They also show you which way to turn next, and they ignite your imagination.

Raise questions:

Constantly create questions to clarify and extend your understanding. What's the real question? Working on the wrong questions can waste a lifetime. Ideas are in the air—the right questions will bring them out and help you see connections that otherwise would have been invisible.

Follow the flow of ideas:

Look back to see where ideas came from and then look ahead to discover where those ideas may lead. A new idea is a beginning, not an end. Ideas are rare—milk them. Following the consequences of small ideas can result in big payoffs.

These four building blocks are basic elements for effective thinking, and we devised an easy way for you to remember them. You only need to recall the classical elements that were once believed to be the essential parts of all nature and matter. Those elements, which predated Socrates and influenced Renaissance culture and thought, are Earth, Fire, Air, and Water. So to help trigger your memory and enable you to apply these techniques, we associate each classical element with one of our strategies for effective thinking, learning, and creating:

Earth ↔ Understand deeply

Fire ↔ Make mistakes

Air ↔ Raise questions

Water ↔ Follow the flow of ideas

By mastering these strategies, you can and will *change*. The classical elements of nature included a fifth special element—the *quintessential element*—that was the changeless matter from which all the heavens were made. Ironically, here in our context of thinking and learning, the quintessential element is *change*.

 The Quintessential Element ↔ Change

Change:

> The unchanging element is change—by mastering the first four elements, you can change the way you think and learn. You can always improve, grow, and extract more out of your education, yourself, and the way you live your life. Change is the universal constant that allows you to get the most out of living and learning.

In any movie, play, or literary work, media scholars tell us how to determine who truly is the main character of the story—it's the individual who, by the end, has changed the most. Your life is an exciting journey. When you embrace change, you put yourself front and center by intentionally deciding in which direction you wish your life's drama to unfold. In doing so, *you* become the hero in your own life's adventure.

The chapters ahead unpack the previous sound-bite sentences by more fully describing our five elements of effective thinking. Exercises, action items, illustrations, and stories in each chapter turn these elements into a practical way to vastly improve individuals and organizations.

The elements and exercises provide you with an intellectual GPS to help you navigate through life. We have seen countless inspirational examples of people who flourish well beyond their own expectations. These stories feed our optimistic belief that we all are capable of living our lives far more successfully than we generally do. Our hope is that students will find these elements transformative; instructors will use these lessons to enrich their classes; leaders of society, whether in business, science, politics, or the arts, will employ these strategies to become more innovative; and lifelong learners will apply these principles to better live as ever-evolving students of the world.

How to Read this Book

Your challenge is to make these elements a part of your daily routine. We urge you to read this tiny book slowly and then reread it. In fact, we thought of literally repeating the entire text three times (making the book three times as long); however, our publisher refused to embrace our innovative idea. Instead we suggest three readings, as follows:

*First read: Take it all in and don't mind the details—*Throughout the text, we provide exercises where we invite you to pause, look back, contemplate, and experiment. However, during your first read-through, don't necessarily pause to attempt these exercises. Instead, get a global sense of the entire story we are telling.

*Second read: Give it a test drive—*Return to the beginning and slowly reread the book, this time stopping to think about and to apply the suggestions and exercises to your life.

*Third read: Make it your own—*You have now tried the exercises and reflected on the elements twice. In this third reading, work toward letting those methods become second nature.

We encourage you to revisit chapters again and again—different elements will resonate with you at different times. The more you absorb and practice these elements of thinking, the more you will get out of them.

At the end of this book you will find an invitation to share your own stories of effective thinking at www .elementsofthinking.com. We look forward to hearing from you.

Earth

1. Grounding Your Thinking
Understand Deeply

> **He never did a thing so very bad.**
> **He don't know why he isn't quite as good**
> **As anyone.**
>
> **—From "The Death of the Hired Man" by Robert Frost**

Silas felt the nervous excitement that all students feel as their professor returns graded exams. When Silas saw the red "58%" on the top of his test paper, he was frustrated, annoyed, and bewildered. "I really knew the stuff on the test. I just made a bunch of stupid little mistakes. I really knew it. Really." And he really believed he knew it. Really. Sadly, such unpleasant surprises do not necessarily end after we receive our diplomas. Many people spend their entire careers confidently (and erroneously) thinking they know more and deserve more than their yearly evaluations, salaries, and success seem to reflect.

Understanding is not a yes-or-no proposition; it's not an on-or-off switch. Silas spent hours studying for his test. But he spent that time memorizing facts rather than building a deep understanding. He would have earned a higher grade had he invested the same amount of time mastering the fundamentals, identifying essential themes, attaching each idea to that core structure, and, finally, imagining what surrounds or extends the material he was studying. Instead, Silas's strategy was like that of a well-intentioned elementary school student who meticulously memorizes the mechanics of adding two-digit numbers but has no idea why the process works, and, as a result, finds adding three-digit numbers as alien as visiting another planet. Silas's understanding was, at best, thin and fragile. Even tiny variations threw him, because he viewed his job as pinning down a certain number of isolated facts rather than understanding the meaning and connections of the ideas.

When you learn anything, go for depth and make it rock solid. If you learn a piece of music for the piano, then, instead of just memorizing finger movements, learn to hear each note and understand the structure of the piece. Ask yourself, "Can I play the notes of the right hand while just humming the notes of the left hand?" If you study the Civil War, rather than memorizing some highlights—Lincoln was president; Lee was a general; slavery played a role—you can try to understand the background, competing forces, and evolving social values that ignited the bloody conflict. When you make political decisions, instead of focusing on a candidate's good looks and fifteen-second sound bites, you can objectively learn about the issues and develop your own reasoned opinions.

You *can* understand anything better than you currently do. Setting a higher standard for yourself for what you mean by *understanding* can revolutionize how you perceive the world. The following steps illustrate why a deep understanding is essential to a solid foundation for future thinking and learning.

Understand simple things deeply

The most fundamental ideas in any subject can be understood with ever-increasing depth. Professional tennis players watch the ball; mathematicians understand a nuanced notion of number; successful students continue to improve their mastery of the concepts from previous chapters and courses as they move toward the more advanced material on the horizon; successful people regularly focus on the core purpose of their profession or life. True experts continually deepen their mastery of the basics.

Trumpeting understanding through a note-worthy lesson. Tony Plog is an internationally acclaimed trumpet virtuoso, composer, and teacher. A few years ago we had the opportunity to observe him conducting a master class for accomplished soloists. During the class, each student played a portion of his or her selected virtuosic piece. They played wonderfully. Tony listened politely and always started his comments, "Very good, very good. That is a challenging piece, isn't it?" As expected, he proceeded to give the students advice about how the piece could be played more beautifully, offering suggestions about physical technique and musicality. No surprise. But then he shifted gears.

He asked the students to play a very easy warm-up exercise that any beginning trumpet player might be given. They played the handful of simple notes, which sounded childish compared to the dramatically fast, high notes from the earlier, more sophisticated pieces. After they played the simple phrase, Tony, for the first time during the lesson, picked up the trumpet. He played that same phrase, but when he played it, it was not childish. It was exquisite. Each note was a rich, delightful sound. He gave the small phrase a delicate shape, revealing a flowing sense of dynamics that enabled us to hear meaning in those simple notes. The students' attempts did not come close—the contrast was astounding. The fundamental difference between the true master and the talented students clearly occurred at a far more basic level than in the intricacies of complex pieces. Tony explained that mastering an efficient, nuanced performance of simple pieces allows one to play spectacularly difficult pieces with greater control and artistry.

The lesson was simple. The master teacher suggested that the advanced students focus more of their time on practicing simple pieces intensely—learning to perform them with technical efficiency and beautiful elegance. Deep work on simple, basic ideas helps to build true virtuosity—not just in music but in everything.

What is deep understanding? How can you realize when you don't know something deeply? When the advanced trumpet students played the simple phrase, they played every note and it sounded good to them. Before hearing the contrast between their renditions and the true virtuoso's performance, the students might not have realized that it was possible to play that phrase far, far better.

In everything you do, refine your skills and knowledge about fundamental concepts and simple cases. Once is never enough. As you revisit fundamentals, you will find new insights. It may appear that returning to basics is a step backward and requires additional time and effort; however, by building on firm foundations you will soon see your true abilities soar higher and faster.

▶ *A WAY TO PROVOKE EFFECTIVE THINKING . . .*

Master the basics

Consider a skill you want to improve or a subject area that you wish to understand better. Spend five minutes writing down specific components of the skill or subject area that are basic to that theme. Your list will be a free-flowing stream of consciousness. Now pick one of the items on your list, and spend thirty minutes actively improving your mastery of it. See how working deeply on the basics makes it possible for you to hone your skill or deepen your knowledge at the higher levels you are trying to attain. Apply this exercise to other things you think you know or would like to know.

▶ **Illustration: A student's response in trying to understand basic economics**

Step 1: A brainstorming list of components: *Maximize profits; free markets; supply and demand; equilibrium of supply and demand.* (Note that the student's list is neither organized nor complete, which is great.) Step 2: Improve understanding of *"equilibrium of supply and demand"*: *First, I need to understand what the graphs of the supply and demand curves mean. The horizontal axis is the quantity and the vertical axis is the price; so I see why the demand graph curves down to the right and the supply graph curves up to the right. I think that equilibrium is the point of intersection of those two graphs. But if the quantity level is to the left of that intersection, then the price for demand is higher than the price for supply. I don't know what that means.* (Note that this student successfully identified a lack of understanding of a basic idea, namely, what the supply and demand graphs represent. He now knows what he should work on first. A firm understanding of that basic idea will allow him to progress further and faster in the future.)

. . . UNDERSTAND DEEPLY ◄

The whole of science is merely a refinement of everyday thinking.
   —Albert Einstein

A commonsense approach leads to the core. Many of the most complicated, subtle, and profound ideas arise from looking unmercifully clearly at simple, everyday experiences. Calculus is one of the most influential concepts in history. It has fundamentally changed the way we experience life today—a wide range of technological innovations, from space exploration to plasma TVs, computers, and cell phones, would not exist without calculus. And calculus is based on thinking deeply about simple, everyday motion—like an apple falling from a tree.

In 1665, England suffered an epidemic of bubonic plague. Cambridge University was closed to stem the dreaded disease's spread, so Isaac Newton and the other students were sent home. Newton spent the next two years on his aunt's farm, during which time he formulated the fundamental ideas of calculus and the laws of physics. The famous story about Newton sitting under an apple tree when an apple fell on his head, giving him the idea of universal gravitation and calculus, may be almost literally true. Thinking about the speed of a falling apple can generate the idea of the *derivative*—the profound extension of the basic notion that speed equals distance divided by time. Thinking about how far the apple would fall if you knew its speed at each instant leads to the idea of the *integral*—the abstraction that distance equals speed multiplied by time.

The grandest, most cosmic ideas, such as how the planets move, arise from thinking deeply about an apple beaning Newton. Newton described the universe—the behavior of the sun, planets, and distant stars—using the same laws that describe everyday occurrences like apples falling from trees. The simple and familiar hold the secrets of the complex and unknown. The depth with which you master the basics influences how well you understand everything you learn after that.

Today, when math teachers are asked what makes calculus so difficult to teach, most reply, "My students don't know the basic mathematics that they saw in the eighth or ninth grade." One secret to mastering calculus is to truly master basic algebra. In any class, when preparing for your next exam, make sure you can earn a 100% on all the previous exams—if you can't, then you're not ready for the test looming in your future. Instructors should also embrace this fundamental reality and help their students have a firmer grasp of the basics that preceded the material currently being explored.

To learn any subject well and to create ideas beyond those that have existed before, return to the basics repeatedly. When you look back after learning a complicated subject, the basics seem far simpler; however, those simple basics are a moving target. As you learn more, the fundamentals become at once simpler but also subtler, deeper, more nuanced, and more meaningful. The trumpet virtuoso found limitless beauty in a simple exercise and, in turn, found deep insights into the more interesting difficult pieces.

▶ *A WAY TO PROVOKE EFFECTIVE THINKING . . .*

Ask: **What do you know?**

Do you or don't you truly know the basics? Consider a subject you think you know or a subject you are trying to master. Open up a blank document on your computer. Without referring to any outside sources, write a detailed outline of the fundamentals of the subject. Can you write a coherent, accurate, and comprehensive description of the foundations of the subject, or does your knowledge have gaps? Do you struggle to think of core examples? Do you fail to see the overall big picture that puts the pieces together? Now compare your effort to external sources (texts, Internet, experts, your boss). When you discover weaknesses in your own understanding of the basics, take action. Methodically learn the fundamentals. Thoroughly understand any gap you fill in as well as its surrounding territory. Make these new insights part of your base knowledge and connect them with the parts that you already understood. Repeat this exercise regularly as you learn more advanced aspects of the subject (and save your earlier attempts so that you can look back and see how far you've traveled). Every return to the basics will deepen your understanding of the entire subject.

▶ **Illustration: Voting**

How well do you know the candidates running for office—their records, their positions? Write a list of issues that are important to you. Then list what you believe to be the positions of the candidates on each issue—their stated opinions, their voting records, and their other actions associated with the issue. Most voters will have inaccurate or only meager knowledge, particularly for candidates they don't support. Then look up the actual records and see the differences. Fleshing out your knowledge will lead to more informed decisions—on Election Day and beyond.

. . . *UNDERSTAND DEEPLY* ◄

When faced with a difficult challenge—don't do it! In a speech delivered to Congress on May 25, 1961, John F. Kennedy challenged the country with the words "I believe that this nation should commit itself to achieving the goal, before this decade is out, of landing a man on the Moon and returning him safely to the Earth." On May 26, the National Space Council didn't suit up an astronaut. Instead their first goal was to *hit* the moon—literally. And just over three years later, NASA successfully smashed Ranger 7 into the moon at an impact velocity of 5,861 miles per hour (after the unmanned spacecraft transmitted over four thousand photographs of the lunar surface). It took fifteen ever-evolving iterations before the July 20, 1969, gentle moon landing and subsequent moon walk by the crew of the Apollo 11 spacecraft.

Great scientists, creative thinkers, and problem solvers do *not* solve hard problems head-on. When they are faced with a daunting question, they immediately and prudently admit defeat. They realize that there is no sense in wasting energy vainly grappling with complexity when, instead, they can productively grapple with simpler cases that will teach them how to deal with the complexity to come.

> **If you can't solve a problem, then there is an easier problem you can't solve: find it.**
> **—George Polya**

When the going gets tough, creative problem solvers create an easier, simpler problem that they *can* solve. They resolve that easier issue thoroughly and then study that simple scenario with laser focus. Those insights often point the way to a resolution of the original difficult problem.

Apply this mind-set to your work: when faced with a difficult issue or challenge, do something else. Focus entirely on solving a subproblem that you know you can successfully resolve. Be completely confident that the extraordinarily thorough work that you invest on the subproblem will later be the guide that allows you to navigate through the complexities of the larger issue. But don't jump to that more complex step while you're at work on the subissue. First just try to *hit* the moon . . . walking on its surface is for another day.

Sweat the small stuff

Consider some complex issue in your studies or life. Instead of tackling it in its entirety, find one small element
of it and solve that part completely. Understand the
subissue and its solution backwards and forwards. Understand all its connections and implications. Consider
this small piece from many points of view and in great
detail. Choose a subproblem small enough that you can
give it this level of attention. Only later should you consider how your efforts could help solve the larger issue.

▶ **Illustration: A student's response to this exercise
applied to time management**

Time management is too big an issue for me, so I'll just
focus on getting my homework done. That's still too big
a task, so let me just focus on starting my homework.
I could commit ten minutes right after each lecture to
review class notes and think about the homework assignment. Then five minutes before the next lecture I
could review the notes from the previous lecture—great,
but not always realistic. So to make it practical, when I
return to my room for the night, I'll commit at least ten
minutes to reviewing the class notes of the day and beginning the assigned homework. In fact, my problem is
not just procrastination but focus. Ah ha! So for those
ten minutes, I'll turn off my computer and cell phone and
spend that short uninterrupted time knowing there will

be no distractions. Without text messages and emails, those ten minutes will be qualitatively different from and better than thirty minutes of interrupted time. That weird serenity will bring me to a meditation-like, focused state of mind. And looking at the homework on the day it was assigned—when it's still fresh in my mind—is better than investing the same amount of time the day before the homework is due—when I'd have to spend time just remembering what was going on. Once I've made this little ten-minute practice a daily habit, I'll revisit the larger challenge of time management. (See how this exercise did its job—it brought out some important principles to consider when facing the daunting challenge of time management: the value of uninterrupted, focused time and the value of carving out small regular intervals of time when they will be most effective.)

. . . UNDERSTAND DEEPLY ◄

Clear the clutter—seek the essential

During most of history, when people thought of flight, they thought it was for the birds. And when we visualize flying birds, we see flapping wings. But, as anyone who has flown on an airplane will attest, flapping is not the essence of flight. It's the gentle curve of the top of the wing and the angle at which that wing meets

the wind that matter. The shape and angle of the wing
are the essential features that generate the lift for birds
and the lift for planes. Ignoring the flapping is incredibly difficult, because it's the most conspicuous, loud-
est, and most obvious feature of birds in flight. Avia-
tion pioneers needed great focus to ignore the obvious
flapping and find the subtle essence that enables us
to soar.

Uncover the essence. When faced with an issue that
is complicated and multifaceted, attempt to isolate
the essential ingredients. The essence is not the whole
issue. There is a further step of understanding how the
other features of the situation fit together; however,
clearly identifying and isolating essential principles
can guide you through the morass. The strategy of
clearing the clutter and seeking the essential involves
two steps:

  Step One: Identify and ignore all distracting features
    to isolate the essential core.
  Step Two: Analyze that central issue and apply those
    insights to the larger whole.

Desperately seeking Waldo. In a series of children's
picture books by Martin Handford called *Where's
Waldo?*, each page contains a large image completely

overrun with hundreds of little cartoon figures entangled together. One of the characters is Waldo, who wears a distinctive red-and-white striped shirt and round glasses. Waldo would be easy to find if it were not for the hundreds of other figures on the page. Children enjoy finding Waldo amid the clutter. If the non-Waldo figures were removed, locating Waldo would be trivial (and boring). The challenge comes from the clutter. If you literally clear the clutter from your desk, the remaining items are easy to find. But not only can clearing the clutter expose those things that you know are there; it can reveal the otherwise invisible essence of the situation.

Many real questions are surrounded and obscured by history, context, and adornments. Within that cloud of vaguely related, interacting influences, you need to pluck out the central themes. Often you may be surprised that after you pare down a complex issue to its essentials, the essentials are much clearer and easier to face. Ignoring things is difficult. Often the peripheral clutter is blinking and clanging and trying madly to draw your attention away from what is really going on. By systematically ignoring one distraction after another, you can turn your attention to more central (often initially invisible) themes. After you clear the clutter, what remains will clarify understanding and open the door to creating new ideas. Remember, you may not be able to see everything, but you can certainly ignore most things.

Pablo Picasso, *The Bull* (plates III, IV, VIII, and XI, 1945–46). © 2012 Estate of Pablo Picasso / Artists Rights Society (ARS), New York. Photos of plates III, VIII, and XI: Erich Lessing / Art Resource, NY. Photo of plate IV: Cameraphoto Arte, Venice / Art Resource, NY

There is no abstract art. You must always start with something. Afterward you can remove all traces of reality.

—Pablo Picasso

Picasso's work—just plain bull. In 1945–1946, Pablo Picasso produced a powerful series of drawings of bulls. When you arrange his bulls in order of detail, the most detailed is a realistic drawing of a bull. All the features are there. Then, in a series of eighteen drawings, Picasso step-by-step simplifies the previous image. The shading of the hide vanishes. The details of the muscles disappear. The texture is gone. The three-dimensionality evaporates. By the eighteenth bull, we see a line drawing—a simple image consisting of ten curves and two ovals. But those twelve marks distill the essence of that bull—its strength and masculinity. The clutter is gone; the essence remains. This final image was the only one in the series that Picasso entitled *The Bull*. By systematically cutting away peripheral parts (being careful not to turn the bull into a cow), we force ourselves to appreciate what's important.

▶ *A WAY TO PROVOKE EFFECTIVE THINKING . . .*

Uncover one essential

Consider a subject you wish to understand, and clear the clutter until you have isolated one essential ingredient. Each complicated issue has several possible core ideas. You are not seeking "the" essential idea; you are seeking just one—consider a subject and pare it down to one theme.

In fact, you might perform this exercise on yourself. What do you view as essential elements of you? Isolating those elements can give a great deal of focus to life decisions.

▶ **Illustration: Parenting**

Bringing up children requires making many decisions on a daily basis. Getting advice about every scenario is impractical. Instead, identify one or two essential goals and use them to guide your actions. For example, one goal may be to raise children to become independent thinkers who take personal responsibility for life decisions. That goal would influence your decision if your children repeatedly fail to complete homework assignments. Do you embrace the easier, short-term solution of finishing their homework; or do you take the more difficult approach of encouraging your children to learn for themselves? Having essential goals in mind makes daily decisions clearer. Whether or not you are a parent, this same perspective can help everyone—teachers, students, professionals, businesspeople, and even politicians—make daily decisions that aim toward long-term goals rather than toward short-term goals that may be diversions.

. . . *UNDERSTAND DEEPLY* ◄

Once you have isolated the essential, you have armed yourself with a solid center upon which to build and embellish. The core is not the whole issue, but it is a lodestar that can guide you through turbulent storms and complications. What's core? What's fluff? Find what's at the center and work out from there. You can confidently center yourself.

See what's there

You (and everyone else) have prejudices.
Admit it already and move forward from there.
  —Two anonymous authors (of this book)

We, the authors, have a passion for art, but sadly our enthusiasm far exceeds our talent. Some years ago while I (BURGER) was visiting Denison University in Ohio, I met a studio art professor and thus had a chance to ask an expert about painting. I simply asked the artist, "Tell me one insight into painting." The artist, a bit surprised by the out-of-the-blue request, thought for several moments and then responded, "Shadows are the color of the sky." I didn't really believe him at first. Like most people, I thought shadows were gray or black, but if you look closely, you will see that indeed shadows in the great outdoors do have color—albeit subtle and muted.

This artistic insight struck me as meaningful beyond just looking at shadows. It showed something about seeing, about seeing what is actually there rather than what seems to be there. I had seen shadows every day of my life, but I was wrong about what they really look like. Those colorful shadows gave me a whole new view of the world—a fresh perspective that transcends the art of painting.

Whenever you "see" an issue or "understand" a concept, be conscious of the lens through which you're viewing the subject. You should assume you're introducing bias. The challenge remains to identify and let go of that bias or the assumptions you bring, and actively work to see and understand the subject anew.

Whether it be physical characteristics of what you see, emotional aspects of what you feel, or conceptual underpinnings of what you understand, acknowledging and then letting go of bias and prejudice can lead you to see what's truly there and (often more importantly) to discover what's missing.

Two experiences from two art classes. Studying art can help us see the real world more clearly. Here we recount two brief tales about our own challenges as art history students.

While an undergraduate at Pomona College, I (Starbird) found myself in the back row of a medieval art history course taught by a truly refined scholar who was very old. Students believed that the secret to her nearly infinite knowledge of Gothic cathedrals was that she'd actually been present when they were built. One day in class, the ancient professor showed a slide of a medieval painting, and asked, "Mr. Starbird, what do you see in this painting?"

Of course nothing profound came to mind. The picture just seemed strange—the body parts were distorted and the bright gold halos looked like the arches at McDonald's, which made my stomach growl. But I knew that art was supposed to have "meaning," so I tried to imitate the art analysis that I had heard, and replied, "I think the halo of light represents the circle of life—emerging from the darkness of the primeval void, arcing into a shining glory, and descending again to the abyss of eternity." Without missing a beat, the dignified professor retorted, "Cut the bull and tell us what you see." Not the reaction I expected.

The second incident occurred many years later when the other author (BURGER), as a professor, decided to sit in on a popular introductory art history course at Williams College. The art professor was brilliantly theatrical and the lectures were riveting. Early in the term, the professor projected an image of a monk, his back to the viewer, standing on the shore, looking off into a blue sea and an enormous sky. The professor asked the class, "What do you see?" The darkened auditorium was silent. We looked and looked and thought and thought as hard as possible to unearth the hidden meaning, but came up with nothing—we must have missed it. With dramatic exasperation she answered her own question, "It's a painting of a monk! His back is to us! He is standing near the shore! There's a blue sea and enormous sky!" Hmm . . . why didn't we see it? So as not to bias us, she'd posed the question without revealing the artist or title of the work. In fact, it was Caspar David Friedrich's *The Monk by the Sea* (1808–1810).

To better understand your world, consciously acknowledge what you *actually* see—no matter how mundane or obvious—rather than guess at what you think you are supposed to see. Saying what you actually see forces you to become conscious of what is there and also what is missing. If you see it, then say it; if you don't see it, then don't claim to see it.

Being honest and accurate about what you actually know and don't know forces you to identify and fill gaps in your understanding. It is at the interface between what you actually know and what you don't yet know that true learning and growth occur.

▶ *A WAY TO PROVOKE EFFECTIVE THINKING . . .*

Say it like you see it

Homework assignments, tests, and job-related assessments ask you what you know. Unfortunately, partial credit or social pressure often encourages you to pretend to know a bit more than you actually do. So in the privacy of your own room look at assignments or possible test questions and write down the weaknesses as well as the strengths of what you know and don't know. Deliberately avoid glossing over any gaps or vagueness. Instead boldly assert what is tepid or missing in your understanding. Now take the action of filling in the gaps. Identifying and admitting your own uncertainties is an enormous step toward solid understanding.

▶ Illustration: Communication

If you are writing an essay, read literally what you have written—not what you intended to communicate.

Pretend you don't know the argument you are making and read your actual words. What's confusing and what's missing? If you think you know an idea but can't express it clearly, then this process has identified a gap or vagueness in your understanding. After you admit and address those weaknesses, your exposition will be clearer and more directed to the actual audience. When delivering an address or making a presentation, apply this same process of deliberately listening to the actual words you are speaking rather than what you imagine you are saying.

. . . UNDERSTAND DEEPLY ◀

What everybody believes is not always what's actually true. Commonly held opinions are frequently just plain false. Often we are persuaded by authority and repetition rather than by evidence and reality. This tendency to accept what surrounds us makes it difficult to separate what we really know from what we just believe we know. To illustrate this distinction, let's consider the downfall of gravity.

Around 340 BCE, Aristotle asserted that objects fall at a rate proportional to their weight. In other words, he thought that heavier objects fall faster than lighter ones. People accepted this assertion for two reasons: (1) it sounded reasonable; and (2) Aristotle said it. The combination of reasonableness and authority is a recipe for entrenched bias. People accepted Aristotle's description of falling bodies for nearly two thousand years. Finally, during the sixteenth and seventeenth centuries, people slowly moved from relying on authority to relying on evidence. As often happens in the recounting of history, the reality of incremental progress is replaced by a myth about an instant change in perspective.

In this case, a myth about Galileo condenses an evolving shift in perspective into a single decisive experiment supposedly (but not actually) conducted by Galileo himself. As legend has it, in 1588 Galileo challenged Aristotle's theory about falling bodies by climbing up to the top of the Leaning Tower of Pisa lugging an iron cannon ball and a less weighty wooden ball of equal size. Hopefully after warning passersby below, he simultaneously dropped both balls, and, much to the surprise of many (especially the unsuspecting promenaders who did not hear the warning), the two balls crashed to the ground at the same instant, thus demonstrating that heavier bodies do *not* fall faster. In fact, except for air resistance, bodies fall at the same rate regardless of their weight. The real myth, then and now, is that people would instantly rely on evidence rather than authority.

How can people, for thousands of years, believe false assertions that are easily disproved? Answer: Individuals tend to accept ideas if people they know or respect state or believe those ideas. You need to be very clear about the foundations of your opinions. If you believe something only because another person— even a professor—told you it was so, then you should not view your understanding as rock solid. The Galileo story illustrates the healthy attitude that evidence settles a question, no matter who says the opposite. Search for evidence and don't be satisfied until you know the why.

> **It's not what you don't know that gets you in trouble.**
> **It's what you do know that ain't so.**
>
> **—Will Rogers *or* Mark Twain *or* someone else**

How do you know? Becoming aware of the basis of your opinions or beliefs is an important step toward a better understanding of yourself and your world. Regularly consider your opinions, beliefs, and knowledge, and subject them to the "How do I know?" test. What is the evidence that your understanding is based upon? Become aware of the sources of your opinions. If your sources are shaky, then you might want to be more open-minded to the possibility that your opinion or knowledge might be incorrect. Regularly find cases in which you need to rethink your views.

Opening our minds to counterintuitive ideas can be the key to discovering novel solutions and building deeper understanding, but how can we take advantage of those opportunities? Certainly we are not intentionally closed-minded. So how can we break free of our unintended closed-mindedness and see the world with less bias?

First, we can simply try out alternative ideas hypothetically and temporarily. In other words, don't say, "Okay, I'll change my opinions on health care right now." Instead, say, "For the next day (or even the next twenty minutes), I'll pretend my opinions are the opposite of what I normally believe (even though I know it's nonsense), and see where those new beliefs take me." This strategy allows you to explore ideas without having to overcome deeply ingrained moral or institutional prejudices. Even following ideas that you know are wrong can be illuminating. Because in following the consequences of those "wrong" ideas, you might be led to better understand why your original belief is indeed correct, or you might be led to new and unexpected insights that run counter to your original beliefs.

The twentieth-century physicist Niels Bohr used this process while trying to lead a group of scientists to understand quantum mechanics. Quantum mechanics is a bizarre description of fundamental particles in physics. Its assertions about the nature of nature are strange and run counter to our intuition about the universe. So in trying to decide whether quantum mechanics might be a correct description of our physical world,

Bohr employed a practice of spending one day assuming that quantum mechanics was true and following the implications of that perspective, and then spending the next day assuming that quantum mechanics was false and following the consequences of that view. By alternating his views, he was able to explore each alternative more objectively. (Incidentally, he eventually decided that quantum mechanics was a better description than the alternative theory of the day.)

▶ *A WAY TO PROVOKE EFFECTIVE THINKING . . .*

Try on alternatives and size up the fit

Take some opinion that you hold that other people (those who clearly are wrong) do not hold. Every other hour accept your own current opinion and think about its implications, and on the alternate hours accept the alternative opinion and see where that leads. Try not to be judgmental. Don't resist the alternative views. You are not committing to any change. This exercise has the goal of understanding alternatives more realistically. As a result, you might change an opinion, but more likely you will simply have a better understanding of why the alternative views make sense to others. If an hour is too long a time period, try the challenge in fifteen-minute intervals.

▶ **Illustration: Sit next to the other side**

Attend a meeting or dinner sponsored by a group that has a point of view different from your own. If you're a student and a Republican, attend a Young Democrats Club event. If you're an atheist, attend a Christian Fellowship meeting. You might feel a bit uncomfortable at first, but avoid letting yourself instantly think of refutations. Instead, listen and try to empathize and see a new point of view—and perhaps make a new connection.

. . . UNDERSTAND DEEPLY ◄

See what's missing

Forcing yourself to see what's actually in front of you rather than what you believe you should see is a difficult task. However, an even greater challenge is to see what's missing. One of the most profound ways to see the world more clearly is to look deliberately for the gaps—the *negative space*, as it is called in the art world; that is, the space surrounding the objects or issues of interest. In our daily and intellectual experiences there are gaps of many sorts. If you're studying some body of material, ask yourself to identify those concepts that you truly do not fully understand. Those concepts may, in fact, be ideas that you were supposed to have mastered in an earlier class or at an earlier point in your life. Don't despair. Honestly admitting those gaps in knowledge and understanding is the first important step in attempting to fill them. Of course, a harder question is this: How can you see what's truly invisible?

Add the adjective and uncover the gaps. Let's return to a time in which photographs were not in living color. During that period, people referred to pictures as "photographs" rather than "black-and-white photographs" as we do today. The possibility of color did not exist, so it was unnecessary to insert the adjective "black-and-white." However, suppose we *did* include the phrase "black-and-white" *before* the existence of color photography. By highlighting that reality, we become conscious of current limitations and thus open our minds to new possibilities and potential opportunities.

World War I was given that name only after we were deeply embattled in World War II. Before that horrific period of the 1940s, World War I was simply called "The Great War" or, even worse, "The War to End All Wars." What if we had called it "World War I" back in 1918? Such a label might have made the possibility of a second worldwide conflict a greater reality for governments and individuals, and might have led to better international policy decisions. We become conscious of issues when we explicitly identify and articulate them.

In 1937, Sylvan Goldman, a small grocery store owner, wanted to better understand his shoppers. In describing the buying ability of a customer, he may have thought, "A person can buy only what he or she can carry." Armed with this insight and his desire to enable his customers to buy more, Mr. Goldman took some wooden folding chairs, and affixed wheels to their legs and a basket to their seats. Goldman invented the shopping cart. Not only did the cash start rolling in, but this innovation also led the way for department, retail, electronic, and home-improvement stores of the future to move lots and lots of merchandise. By just describing what was there, he was led to see the invisible.

▶ *A WAY TO PROVOKE EFFECTIVE THINKING . . .*

See the invisible

Select your own object, issue, or topic of study and attach an adjective or descriptive phrase (such as "the First" before "World War") that points out some reality of the situation, ideally some feature that is limiting or taken for granted. Then consider whether your phrase suggests new possibilities or opportunities. It might be helpful to think of this exercise as a word-association game. For example, if you are a student, you could consider a word such as "semester" and then list the first few adjectives that come to mind—for example "busy," "boring," "tiring," "exciting," and the like. Use your newfound adjectives to create interesting and provocative insights that might otherwise have gone unnoticed.

▶ Illustration: An education

Caroline was contemplating issues in the field of education and decided to apply the "include the adjective" exercise. She quickly described the current educational system as "nonindividualized education." That designation immediately made her wonder about the extent to which education could—perhaps in the future—be tailored to individual differences in learning styles, in what each individual knows, in goals for education, and so forth. These thoughts were all inspired by just her description of how we teach today.

. . . UNDERSTAND DEEPLY ◀

Final thoughts: Deeper is better

"Understand deeply" is great advice, but what does it really mean? The truth is that most of us never understand anything deeply. After not doing well on a test, students often tell us, "I knew it, but I couldn't explain it . . . ," to which we respond, "If you can't explain it, you don't know it."

Understanding simple things deeply means mastering the fundamental principles, ideas, and methods that then create a solid foundation on which you can build. Seeking the essential creates the core or skeleton that supports your understanding. Seeing what's actually there without prejudice lets you develop a less biased understanding of your world. And seeing what's missing helps you to identify the limits of your knowledge, to reveal new possibilities, and to create new solutions to complex problems. From the physical world to society, academics, personal relations, business, abstract ideas, and even sports, a deep examination of the simple and familiar is a potent first step for learning, thinking, creating, and problem solving.

Though "seeing deeply" is a valuable metaphor, it's also a literal reality when we look at the familiar world under magnification. When we focus a magnifying glass, and then a microscope, on ordinary objects, we suddenly see not only new worlds, but also explanations and organizing principles for our original, macroscopic world. In fact, we associate understanding with the element Earth because when we attain a rich understanding, we are literally standing upon rock-solid, firm ground. Earth is that which is *under* where we *stand*.

When you look at your own familiar world with unaccustomed depth and clarity, that world will open up to show richness, structure, and meaning that you never saw before. Among the goals of this book are to describe how you can construct original ideas, to show how you can solve old problems, and to reveal how you can create new worlds. Here we are advocating a process that starts with your most comfortable surroundings, your most familiar territory, the basics that you know best, and encourages you to search deeply for features that you don't ordinarily perceive.

This strategy opens your mind to success in everything from conquering calculus and producing provocative essays to everything beyond.

What you know most about in this world are the familiar objects, actions, and ideas that make up the vast majority of your life experience. But what you don't do regularly is examine those common features of your life with a probing mind. You can intentionally look at familiar objects, actions, ideas, and experiences unusually deeply. And when you do, your voyage of discovery will begin. The familiar is full of unseen depth and wonder. Clear away the distractions, see what's actually there, and make the invisible visible.

Fire

2. Igniting Insights through Mistakes
Fail to Succeed

> **Success is the ability to go from one failure to another with no loss of enthusiasm.**
> **—Winston Churchill**

Back in the 1970s three young guys (one being a college dropout) saw a chance to make it big. They put the rubber to the road and created a company that would efficiently analyze automobile traffic data collected from pneumatic road tube counters—and gave their new venture the catchy company name Traf-O-Data. How could it fail? Although they produced some fine hardware and software, they ended up generating just a few thousand dollars in revenue, and quickly admitted defeat and closed the fledgling business. It was a failure. But through that failed enterprise those techno-geeks gained considerable and profound insights into computing machines and their true potential. Two of those founders took what they'd learned from their failed attempt and launched another start-up company—this time, with the catchy name Microsoft. Paul Allen and Bill Gates are poster boys for the power of exploiting failure and allowing mistakes to lead the way.

"Fail" is not an obscene word. In our society "fail" is viewed as another offensive four-letter word beginning with "f." The typical attitude that mistakes should be avoided is patently wrong and has several detrimental consequences. The mind-set that mistakes are poisonous often freezes us into inaction. If we have the healthier attitude that failure is a potent teacher and a scheduled stop along the road to success, then we find ourselves liberated to move forward sooner, because mistakes are actions we definitely can take at any time. If you're stuck, a mistake can be just the thing to unstick you.

Any creative accomplishment evolves out of lessons learned from a long succession of missteps. Failure is a critical element of effective learning, teaching, and creative problem solving. Mistakes direct our attention in productive ways by forcing us to focus on the specific task of determining why the attempt at hand failed. Effective failure is an important, positive (and, as in the case of Microsoft, lucrative) step toward success.

Viewing failure as an opportunity for learning requires a fresh mind-set. If you think, "I'm stuck and giving up. I know I can't get it right," then get it wrong. Once you make the mistake, you can ask, "Why is *that* wrong?" Now you're back on track, tackling the original challenge.

Students need to experience the arc of starting with failure and ending with success. Teachers need to embrace the power of failure by consciously inspiring students to learn the productive potential of making mistakes as important steps toward understanding.

▶ *A WAY TO PROVOKE EFFECTIVE THINKING . . .*

Fail nine times

The next time you face a daunting challenge, think to yourself, "In order for me to resolve this issue, I will have to fail nine times, but on the tenth attempt, I will be successful." This attitude frees you and allows you to think creatively without fear of failure, because you understand that learning from failure is a forward step toward success. Take a risk and when you fail, no longer think, "Oh, no, what a frustrating waste of time and effort," but instead extract a new insight from that misstep and correctly think, "Great: one down, nine to go—I'm making forward progress!" And indeed you are. After your first failure, think, "Terrific, I'm 10% done!" Mistakes, loss, and failure are all flashing lights clearly pointing the way to deeper understanding and creative solutions.

▶ **Illustration: The authors' response**

We see ourselves as teachers of effective thinking. As such, we are so committed to failure that we assess and reward it. In our classes, 5% of our students' course grades is based on their quality of failure. You want an A in our classes? You had better fail and fail productively, that is, learn through those failed efforts. Every mistake is a teacher and holds a lesson. When you are working on problems that have not yet been solved, there are no guarantees about how soon you will find answers. The unknown solutions may be miles and years away, or you might be surprised to find them tomorrow right around the corner.

. . . FAIL TO SUCCEED ◀

The moral of this chapter's story is that mistakes are positive elements of quintessential thinking and failure is an important part of the foundation upon which to build success.

> **I've missed more than 9,000 shots in my career. I've lost almost 300 games. 26 times, I've been trusted to take the game winning shot and missed. I've failed over and over and over again in my life. And that is why I succeed.**
> **—Michael Jordan**

Once you're open to the positive potential of failure, failing productively involves two basic steps: *creating the mistake* and then *exploiting the mistake*.

In this chapter we encourage you to embrace several facets of failure that can lead to success. One method is to try your best to get it right and, if and when you fail, isolate the specific failed features of that attempt. Alternatively, deliberately try something that you know is wrong to identify and clarify specifically where the defects lie. Analyze each specific mistake to understand the reason it's wrong, thus gaining new insights that may point you in the right direction. Finally, examine the mistakes to see whether the failed attempt might be a correct solution to a different problem.

Welcome accidental missteps—let your errors be your guide

A specific mistake is an excellent source of insight and direction, because a mistake gives you something specific to think about: "This attempt is wrong because ——." When you fill in the blank, you are forcing yourself to identify precisely what is wrong with your attempted solution. This process shifts the activity from trying to think of a *correct* solution, which you don't know at the moment, to the activity of *correcting* mistakes, which is often something you can do.

Mary does mathematics. Mary was a first-year art and literature student in an Honors Program at The University of Texas. Much to her horror, the Honors

Program had a mathematics requirement and Mary was forced to enroll in a course appearing in the catalog as Modern Mathematics. She found herself in my (STARBIRD'S) section of the class. Mary, along with many of her fellow students, was taking this class for one reason: she was forced to. She was truly excellent at many things, but she was not interested in math; in fact, she hated the subject. Not surprisingly, she was largely disengaged from the class discussions. She was going through the motions only to fulfill what she saw as an unnecessary requirement, check it off her to-do list, and quickly move on. This attitude should never offend an instructor, because hopefully that instructor has his or her own goals for the class—in this case, not to create math converts, but instead to offer students an experience that could, in fact, transform their lives in a positive way both in and beyond their formal education. This is Mary's story.

One day, during a discussion about infinity—an abstract and counterintuitive subject that is challenging even for advanced math students—I posed a deep and subtle question. I knew that this question was beyond the reach of the students in my class, so I told them that they would not be able to completely answer the question. Nevertheless, I wanted them to think about the issue as best they could. I instructed them to work in small groups to discuss the question and come up with some attempt at an answer. After about three minutes, I brought the small-group discussions to a close and asked to hear their ideas. As a rule, instead of asking for volunteers, I "cold-call" and pick my own volunteers, and, on that day, I picked Mary.

It was clear that Mary was uneasy to hear her name called. When I asked her for her answer, she replied, "I don't want to say it, because I know it's wrong." Trying to be encouraging and supportive, I agreed with her: "I'm sure it's wrong, but I still want to hear it." She then, reluctantly and with considerable annoyance, described her attempt. As she did, I wrote her solution on the blackboard. When she was through, I congratulated her, "You're right—your solution is wrong!" The entire class laughed and even Mary smiled momentarily. "But I've already told you that no one would figure it out. Now Mary, tell me just one thing that is wrong with your answer." Mary was able to quickly and clearly articulate something that was missing from her answer. I then prompted her: "Great! Now how can you expand your incomplete solution to remove that specific defect you mentioned?" In a perfect *Jeopardy!* response she asked, "Couldn't we just . . . ?" and offered a small modification of her original attempt that fixed the defect she had detected.

"Great! Now Mary, is *this* solution correct?" To which she quickly answered, "No."

"Great! So Mary, tell me just one thing that is wrong with your current answer." She did.

"Great! Now fix your incomplete solution to remove as many defects as you can find." Adapting the method that fixed the first defect, she quickly fixed several more and explained to the class her modified answer.

"Great! Now Mary, is *this* solution correct?" To which she triumphantly answered, "Yes!" But another student piped up and pointed out that there were still some omissions. To which Mary responded, "Shoot," or words to that effect.

I said, "Okay, continue on. Find an error and fix it." After five iterations of this process of finding an error and fixing it, Mary realized that she was getting closer and closer to a complete, correct answer. For the sixth time, I asked, "Is *this* solution correct?" With great confidence and pride Mary answered, "*Yes, it is!*"

And it *was* correct; moreover, the solution she'd discovered was creatively different from the standard answer found in math textbooks, including the textbook that we had authored. Mary created her own ideas to answer the question. My entire contribution was to ask her to make a guess, ask whether that guess was correct, ask for a specific defect of the attempt, ask her to fix that particular flaw, and repeat the process.

As class let out that day, Mary approached me and told me that after our little back-and-forth exercise, her mind was reeling. She had an essay due in her English class that she was stuck on. Now she knew exactly what to do. She would just sit down and write a really bad draft and then look for problems and fix them. There was a specific action she could definitely take. She could make a mistake. She felt liberated.

Mary's story is thought provoking. She had resolved a difficult issue that was by all measures well beyond her abilities. She used a technique of thinking that made her creative, effective, and successful. There is no vagueness or uncertainty about having solved this mathematical challenge. She definitely could not have done it without help; but the help was not mathematical. The help was entirely about how to engage her mind. And, of course, she could have used that exact same technique by simply giving herself the same prompts: make an attempt, find a flaw, fix it, make an attempt . . . She could have been her own teacher. Furthermore, she can apply that technique to anything she wishes.

Mary's story illustrates one specific, practical, broadly applicable strategy for effective thinking, learning, and creating. Successful students and famously successful people have used this strategy throughout history, and you can use it for your own benefit.

Missteps in history. Why do speeches, music, art, architecture, software, books, and plays all require first drafts? Because it's not until Shakespeare reads his bad first draft that he will discover what's really rotten in the state of Denmark. The defects as well as the strengths of our first effort aren't available for us to examine until they exist. Making the errors overt makes the corrections overt as well. Moreover, drafts often contain unexpected strong features. Iteration allows us to see what's there and how we can improve—a little bit at a time.

On December 8, 1941, Franklin Delano Roosevelt delivered to Congress and the American people one of the most important speeches of his presidency. The first line of his oration was so powerful that many still remember his words: "Yesterday, December 7th, 1941—a date which will live in infamy—the United States of America was suddenly and deliberately attacked by naval and air forces of the Empire of Japan." Those perfectly chosen words did not arrive all at once. They evolved from an earlier typed draft—a draft that FDR himself edited in his own hand. That earlier opening line read, "Yesterday, December 7, 1941, a date which will live in world history, the United States of America was simultaneously and deliberately attacked by naval and air forces of the Empire of Japan without warning." Great speeches become great only after they have had the opportunity first to be, well, not so great.

A man's errors are his portals of discovery.

    —James Joyce

First drafts are not just for writers. Thomas Edison was famous for his incremental approach to intentional invention: try something; see what's wrong; learn from the defect; try again. When he said that invention is 1% inspiration and 99% perspiration, the perspiration was the process of incrementally making mistakes and learning from them to make the next attempts apt to be closer to right. When Edison was asked how he felt about his countless failed attempts at making a light-bulb, he replied, "I have not failed. I've just found 10,000 ways that won't work."

Success is not about almost always succeeding. How would you feel if you were failing about 60% of the time? Sounds like a solid "F." Well, in certain contexts you'd be a superstar. A major league baseball player who failed 60% of the time—that is, who had a batting average of .400—would be phenomenal. No living player is that good. So in baseball, every player fails far more than half the time. In mathematical or scientific research, the batting averages are dramatically lower still. If scientists or mathematicians answer even one truly significant question in their whole life, they will be rightly regarded with great esteem. Success is about persisting through the process of repeatedly failing and learning from failure.

The American Constitution has been a model for many governments around the world. But how many people remember that this was version 2.0? The Founding Fathers' first attempt at government, namely, the Articles of Confederation, failed. The Articles of

Confederation represented an attempt to organize the newly independent American states. When the Articles of Confederation were written, the authors did not view that attempt as a temporary measure until something better came along. The authors were striving for a long-term government. However, the defects of the Articles of Confederation provided valuable insights that led to the Constitution of the United States. And, of course, even our treasured Constitution has amendments, each correcting a defect or adding an improvement. Creating a solution and then identifying its limitations leads to further refined solutions.

> **The way to get good ideas is to get lots of ideas and throw the bad ones away.**
>
>   **—Linus Pauling**

You may not know how to do it right, but you can certainly do it wrong. A good way to generate useful mistakes is simply to tackle the issue at hand by quickly constructing the best solution you can with little or no effort. Like magic, suddenly many useful errors will appear. Here's a practical means by which to create ideas.

Don't stare at a blank screen

Take an issue or problem you are facing. For example, you may want to get organized or write a business plan or improve a course grade or write an essay or get more out of life. Open up a blank document on your computer. Now just quickly type *any* ideas—good, bad, inaccurate, or vague—that you have about the issue. Don't hesitate to record ideas or phrases that you know are not quite right—no one (except you) is going to read what you write. Your ideas will be very bad in many ways. They will be disorganized and jumbled. They will be inaccurate or simply wrong. They'll be impractical. They will be boring. They won't come close to resolving the issue. They won't be creative. Congratulations—excellent start!

You may not feel that writing down bad ideas is a worthwhile start, but one thing is certain: writing down bad ideas is something *anyone* can do. Anyone at any time can write a truly awful letter, report, essay, or story. Anyone can write down specific approaches to a problem that don't work. That is not a challenge. But it's also not the end of the story.

Now read what you wrote and focus on two features: *what's right* and *what's wrong*. When you just write down ideas without worrying about correctness, structure, or elegance, your thoughts about the subject often flow out freely and clearly. The ideas that you are trying to express are in you, so when you write without fretting about the mistakes, the surprising reality is that you will often say what you really want to say. You will include partial truths as well as some unexpected gems. Now you have something to do. You can tease out the good elements. You might find particularly nice phrases or pieces of strong ideas. You might uncover a word that is suggestive of some unstated interesting notion. You might find that you have clarified for yourself the core of the idea that you want to express. Looking for good features in your bad first attempt is a great first step toward some creative, high-quality work.

Next, see if you can recognize and exploit what's wrong. When something is bad, it's often easy to see what's wrong and identify mistakes. Now you have something to do: correct the errors you see. You are no longer staring at a blank computer screen hoping for perfection to magically materialize. You have created ideas and put them out where you can see them. You have traded in the impossible task of creating something that's perfect for the much easier task of mining gems and correcting errors. You are now doing something different—you are not creating a work on a blank canvas but instead you are responding to a work already there. Your responses, in turn, will lead to new good ideas that you could not have created before you made the requisite mistakes. In making this action item practical, you must be sure to give yourself enough time for the required iterations. Thus you must commit to starting your effort (that is, creating a crummy draft or first attempt) far enough in advance to allow the necessary gestation and iteration that leads to a polished work of which you will be proud. So start early.

▶ **Illustration: This book**
   You're holding the result of many applications of this exercise.

. . . FAIL TO SUCCEED ◀

In my (BURGER'S) sophomore year at Connecticut College, I experienced a profound exercise in an introductory philosophy class taught by Professor Lester Reiss. In the middle of the semester Reiss gave the instructions for the first major essay. We were to write an essay not to exceed five pages; he gave no other specific instructions, except the title of the essay itself: "My View of the World." This was a daunting but terrific exercise in taking all the great ancient philosophers we had studied thus far and filtering their ideas through our minds. Then, as the end of the term was looming, Professor Reiss gave us the instructions for the final ten-page essay. Again he simply gave us its title: "My View of the World." That opportunity to revisit my own ideas from two months earlier and see how my mind had changed was a powerful exercise that remains with me as an important lesson. In fact, I incorporate this profound idea in my own classes on mathematics by asking students to regularly revisit concepts they've previously considered. Create such opportunities for yourself whether or not you're a student. Allow work to grow and evolve through iteratively identifying and improving on previous drafts and missteps.

Give credit to failure. Instructors need to celebrate students' useful missteps, because those failed attempts lead to important epiphanies at the end. For example, if an instructor gives a cumulative final examination, then why not allow that grade to replace an earlier exam grade if the score on the final is higher? Why are we punishing students for their intermediate missteps that are, in fact, essential for the learning process? And why not embrace a similar mind-set in the professional and business worlds?

If at first you do succeed, try, try again (until you finally fail). In our own classes, we often intentionally solicit student mistakes. First, we ask our students to present their solutions to the entire class. If a student presents a correct solution, we will sometimes ask for another volunteer to present an *erroneous* solution to the same challenge, so the class can explore the reasons behind that defect. Understanding what doesn't work and why is valuable knowledge. This procedure validates the importance and positive value of making mistakes as a means of moving forward toward a deeper understanding of a body of knowledge.

Students need to learn and grow from their intermediate failures. If a student does poorly on an assignment, then burying it in the back of a notebook is foolish failure. This student has been given a great gift—the gift of being told what is wrong. Now it is the student's responsibility—if that individual is interested in truly succeeding—to make that wrong a right. How? By revisiting—right then and there (not the day before the test)—those ideas that are not yet rock solid. Students often say, "I got an 80% on this homework; that's good enough and I'm moving on." Bad idea. By not exploiting this great opportunity to learn from their mistakes, they're essentially throwing away—on average—20% of their grade on their next exam *before* they've even taken it, and they're building future work on a cracked foundation. Why not learn from your current missteps today and give yourself a 20% bonus in your future? Mistakes present a great opportunity to learn and improve, but action is required. The wise instructor (or organizational leader) will clearly make it worthwhile for a student (or member of the group)—right then and there—to learn from the mistakes. To make failure a positive step toward success, you need to revise your work, try again, try more, and seek help until you've completely understood the defects in your failed efforts.

**Ever tried. Ever failed. No matter. Try again. Fail again.
Fail better.**

   —Samuel Beckett

Finding the right question to the wrong answer

Sometimes when your attempt fails to resolve one
issue, you might discover that you have actually found
an imaginative answer to a totally different question.
That is, your bad solution to one problem might lead
to a different project altogether—a project suggested
by the accidental virtues of your mostly bad attempt.

Junk bonds. At 3M Research Laboratories, if someone says "scotch," coworkers think "transparent tape"
rather than "adult beverage"—and for good reason:
3M is one of the leading manufacturers of all that is
sticky. In 1970, 3M scientist Spencer Silver was working hard to create an even stronger adhesive. His creation was a resounding failure. In fact, the bond was
actually *weaker* than other 3M products of the day—it
was so weak it could be stuck to objects and then easily lifted off them without a trace. Oh, well. Silver did
not come unglued over his failed attempt, and 3M did
not fire him. Wise move, since four years later, when
3M scientist Arthur Fry was trying to devise a way
of placing bookmarks in his hymnal so they would
neither fall out nor damage the pages, he recalled

his colleague's weak mixture. Fry coated part of his bookmarks with Silver's superweak adhesive and thus accidentally gave birth to one of 3M's most lucrative products: the Post-it note. It all arose out of a failed attempt.

Seeing a mistake as possibly a correct answer to a different question puts our thinking on its head. We look at a mistake not as a wrong answer, but instead as an opportunity to ask, "What is the question to which this is a correct answer?"

Two reactions to mistakes. So when you see or make a mistake, you have at least two actions to take: (1) let the mistake lead you to a better attempt, and/or (2) ask whether the mistake is a correct answer to a different question.

▶ *A WAY TO PROVOKE EFFECTIVE THINKING . . .*

Have a bad day

Bad days happen to good people. What separates the good from the great is how we react to that bad day. Bad days often include uncomfortably clear lessons about how to grow, learn, or reassess. So the next time you're having a bad day, make the conscious effort to find and extract positive lessons from those not-so-positive experiences.

▶ **Illustration: Have a "Mary Day"**

Was Mary's day in her math class a good day or a bad one? At first blush it seemed not to be going well—the class was discussing "infinity," which is scary enough, but then she was called out to share her thinking. That thinking was not perfect. However, by embracing her weaknesses as a way to reflect and learn, she grew. By the end of the class, Mary had created something new and learned an important lesson about how to create ideas in the future—she had a bad day and, by taking advantage of it, made it a great one.

. . . FAIL TO SUCCEED ◄

Failing by intent

Going to the extreme. Now we take the act of failing to its extreme: One profound way to make new discoveries is to *intentionally* fail along the way. Deliberately exaggerating or considering extreme, impractical scenarios often frees us to have an unforeseen insight. For example, manufacturers conduct stress tests to the point of breaking a product. Studying when and how the product fails provides valuable information on its relative strengths and weaknesses.

Here is an example inspired by a middle school teacher. She was asked how she would teach some ideas of geometry if she had no constraints at all—that is, suppose she had unlimited resources and plenty of time and support. Her response was that she would take her entire class to the Eiffel Tower and measure its height using angles to illustrate the importance of similar triangles. Taking her class to Paris is totally ridiculous and out of the question. However, her solution, which she knew was impractical, actually leads directly to a very important epiphany. Namely, why not leave the classroom? Take the students outside so that they realize that mathematics is about the world around them, not just something you do inside the confines of the textbook. This important insight came from a solution that the teacher knew was impractical when she offered it.

In business, you could ask what you would do if there were no budgetary constraints whatsoever. Maybe some aspects of those unrealistic solutions will point the way toward a practical solution that you otherwise would never have even considered.

Have you ever tried to solve one of those challenging metal tavern puzzles in which you must get one piece disentangled from the rest of the puzzle? One effective method for making progress is to pretend the puzzle is completely elastic. Then you can usually imagine rather easily how to disentangle the pieces. Having learned the steps required to solve the rubber version of the puzzle, you can see what needs to be done with the rigid pieces to accomplish the same outcome. Solving the much easier but clearly unrealistic puzzle has transformed the difficult challenge into two conceptual steps—how to solve the easier rubber version of the puzzle, and then how to translate each of those steps to the unbending metal pieces.

Some artistic movements—such as minimalism—were iconic examples of artists' exaggerating a feature to extremes. Some viewers might look upon the results as mistakes, although the artists might view the results as plumbing the depths of artistic expression. Either way, exploring extremes is illuminating. An effective strategy for gaining insight is to exaggerate conditions either through a physical or a thought experiment.

▶ *A WAY TO PROVOKE EFFECTIVE THINKING . . .*

Exaggerate to generate errors

Consider an issue or problem and now exaggerate some feature of it to a ridiculous extreme. For example, take a political, personal, business, academic, or other issue and create an extremely exaggerated perspective on the subject. If you are arguing one side of an issue (whether or not it is the side you truly believe), make the argument so exaggerated that you realize that it's way over the top. Now study your exaggerated description and discover some underlying defect. Does that defect exist in your original, nonexaggerated perspective? You might apply this exercise to such things as organizational structures or sports or any other activity or belief. As if you were conducting a stress test, you might apply this exercise to something that works well and learn how it breaks down. For example, large companies hire hackers to attempt to break into their computer systems to expose security weaknesses.

Alternatively, try exaggerating a character (fictional or historical) or circumstance far beyond what you think a reader would tolerate. When you read your sketch, you might discover that vast exaggeration is closer to what you want than you could possibly have guessed, but, in any case, the exaggeration might give you a new insight into the role of the character or circumstance in your own mind.

The strategy of exaggeration to extremes can be applied to any issue, from writing to marketing to product development to politics. You might perform this exercise physically or metaphorically, depending on the issue.

▶ Illustration 1: In business

Jones & Sons Lawn Care business is failing owing to the success of its main competitor, Green Thumb Cutters. The ridiculous extreme fantasy is to have the competition disappear. How can that silly fantasy help Jones & Sons? One way to make that Green Thumb go away is to acquire it and thus remove it as a competitor. Alternatively, one could make a competitor disappear by creating products or services that complement the other business—that is, rather than compete with the prosperous company, consider ways of sharing in its success. For example, Jones & Sons could lease and maintain lawn mowers for Green Thumb.

▶ **Illustration 2: In school**

Suppose a student's tendency is to cram and begin working on homework assignments at the last minute. An extreme stance would be to imagine starting an assignment at the first minute, that is, at the moment it is assigned. While this proposal may not be practical, it does lead us to an important insight: *When* you complete an assignment impacts what you can gain from that exercise. A student gets more out of completing homework earlier than out of doing so later, even if the time spent in each case is the same.

. . . FAIL TO SUCCEED ◀

Learning from other's missteps. Often we don't even have to be the ones to actually make the mistake. We all know that some of our greatest lessons were learned from some of the worst people. When we see an evil or inept person in action, or we see a good or competent person make a huge blunder, we find it easy to recognize the pitfall and consciously turn that moment into a learning opportunity.

Final thoughts: A modified mind-set

Mistakes and failure are not signs of weakness; instead they are opportunities for future success. Failure is a sign of a creative mind, of original thought and strength. In fact, at Williams College one of the authors created a course entitled Exploring Creativity, in which students found themselves facing unfamiliar and uncomfortable intellectual challenges. To succeed in that course, students were required to push themselves hard to take risks and create wildly without fear of failure. A person who is willing to fail is someone who is willing to step outside the box. Being willing to fail is a liberating attribute of transformative thinking. Failing is progress; it's not losing ground. Often a mistake or the revelation of error is the most important step toward success. A colossal error may be just millimeters away from a great insight.

When you're stuck, and you don't know what to do, don't do nothing—instead, fail. Making a specific mistake puts you in a different and better position than you were in before you started. And it's a forward step you know you can actually take.

A ship in port is safe, but that's not what ships are built for.

—Admiral Grace Murray Hopper

Let's be honest: failure can be frightening and uncomfortable—a true trial by fire. Thus it is with the element Fire that we associate the strategy of failing on the way to succeeding. Problems that require truly creative solutions are problems that you simply do not yet know how to solve. This book is all about being successful—even if and often because you fail first.

Air

3. Creating Questions out of Thin Air
Be Your Own Socrates

The unexamined life is not worth living.

—Socrates

Many people view questions as irksome—they associate questions with being ignorant, being lost, or, even worse, being tested. But here we suggest a different perspective and show that questions can be an inspiring guide to insight and understanding. In fact, the very act of *creating* questions, for yourself, is a profound step toward understanding—even if the questions are neither asked nor answered.

Socrates is perhaps the most famous philosopher in human history because of his method of generating ideas. He challenged his students, friends, and even enemies to make new discoveries by asking them uncomfortable, core questions. You would certainly be astonishingly successful if you had your very own personal Socrates with you at all times, prodding you with the right leading questions. In fact, such a

24/7 Socrates *is* possible, because you *can* generate your own questions that challenge your own assumptions and lead to insights. You *can* become your own Socrates.

Wisdom just for the asking. Traditionally people believe that it's in the answering of questions that progress is made. In fact, creating questions is as important as answering them, if not more so, because framing good questions focuses your attention on the right issues. Remember how Mary, from the previous chapter, devised an original answer to a question about infinity not only by making mistakes, but by repeatedly considering the basic questions: "Is your solution correct?" and "How can you improve your solution?"—two questions that Mary could easily have raised on her own.

Constantly formulating and raising questions is a mind-opening habit that forces you to have a deeper engagement with the world and a different inner experience. Asking yourself challenging questions can help you reveal hidden assumptions, avoid bias, expose vagueness, identify errors, and consider alternatives. Generating questions can help direct your next steps toward deeper understanding and creative problem solving.

How answers can lead to questions

Every scenario and circumstance can provoke an endless list of valuable questions. Asking questions should not be reserved for moments when you don't know an answer. Even when you do know the answer, asking, "What if . . . ?" is a great way to see more and delve deeper. If you gained nothing else from your formal education but the mind-set of always asking, "What if . . . ?" then you would have benefited tremendously from your schooling. "What if . . . ?" questions invite you to see the world differently because those questions force you to challenge the status quo and to explore the limits of your understanding. The habit of framing questions helps you see what's missing and thus see what needs creating.

A tragic challenge. On January 28, 1986, there was a catastrophic failure during the launch of the space shuttle *Challenger* that resulted in an explosive disaster. There was a subsequent probe (a probe, as a topical aside, means "a process of learning by questioning") by a presidential commission, whose members included the famous theoretical physicist Richard Feynman from Caltech. One of the key facts of the disaster was the unusually low air temperature the night before the launch. In the videos of the launch, moments before liftoff there appeared a slight misalignment between two parts of the solid rocket booster. This observation moved the investigation to the O-ring seals used between the segments of the boosters.

These engineering issues are extremely complex and involve chemistry, physics, and mechanics. But Dr. Feynman cut right to the heart of the issue by simply asking, "What if we just test the elasticity of a cooled O-ring?" In fact, he conducted a simple demonstration live on the televised broadcast of the investigation. He took one of NASA's O-rings, clamped it down with a little C-clamp, and submerged it in a paper cup filled with ice water. When he removed the C-clamp, the entire coast-to-coast audience could see that the cold rubber did not return to its previous round shape. The miserable mystery was solved.

Confident leaders in every profession are not afraid to ask the stupid questions. "Stupid," of course, is not the appropriate adjective for these questions—we actually mean *basic* questions: the questions to which you may feel embarrassed about not already knowing the answers. A transformative but challenging personal policy is to never pretend to know more than you do. Don't build on ambiguity and ignorance. When you don't know something, admit it as quickly as possible and immediately take action—ask a question.

If you have forgotten who the governor is or how many hydrogen atoms are in a molecule of water (H_2O), or what 7×8 is, just make a joke about yourself or quietly ask a friend, but one way or the other quit hiding, and take action. Paradoxically, when you ask basic questions, you will more than likely be perceived by others to be smarter. And more importantly, you'll end up knowing far more over your lifetime. This approach will cause you to be more successful than you would have been had you employed the common practice of pretending to know more than you do. Effective teachers encourage, invite, and even force their students to ask those fundamental questions. Insightful questions, such as "What happens if we put a clamped O-ring in a cup of ice water?" can change the world.

Overcoming bias. Do you remember that shadows are the color of the sky? That counterintuitive reality reminds us that preconceived notions, bias, and prejudice color our view of the world. One profound habit of thinking individuals is to first acknowledge their biases and then intentionally overcome them. Asking challenging questions can help. Passionately argue an issue from the opposite point of view, and ask probing and difficult questions that challenge your original stance. Be brutally honest and see what's actually there rather than what's expected. Get in the habit of asking, "Do I really *know*?" and refuse to accept assertions blindly. Challenge everything and everyone—including your teachers. Don't be intimidated. You are the best authority on what you don't understand—trust yourself: don't be afraid to ask the questions you need to ask, and be brave enough to change your thinking when you uncover a blind spot.

Take another look. Get in the habit of asking how the issue looks from various viewpoints. Frame questions in different ways. Alternative perspectives lead to new sights and new insights. With mathematical questions, you can think about the issues numerically, graphically, algebraically, or physically. With social issues, you can think of them economically, globally, locally, and historically. Moreover, we can investigate issues from an evolutionary point of view and ask what is causing change; how those influences have caused change over time; and how they will cause change in the future. Try to bridge ideas from one discipline or area to another. Ask whether the skills, attitudes, techniques from one subject might be applied to another subject and to your work or life. In our experience, the students who embraced this mind-set have far outperformed—not just in their classes, but in their lives beyond school—those who dismissed this point of view. Everything fits together and interacts—take the transformative step of asking how.

If an exam is looming in your future, prepare by writing the test itself. Well beforehand, compose a list of good exam questions, put it away for a few days, and then later dig it out and take that mock test. Contemplating questions that you think *should* appear on the test will force you to ask, "What are the central ideas here and do I truly understand them?" And metaphorically write your own exam in other circumstances in which you are sharing information or skills, such as in preparing for an interview or a presentation. This "create-a-test" exercise is an excellent one to employ before you face an audience for a Q&A session. Do you know the material so well that you know what the good questions are? If you don't, then you do not understand the material well enough, and you need to go deeper. The questions will help you uncover weak points as well as place what you are saying into a larger context. Remember: If you can't create the questions, you're not ready for the test.

▶ *A WAY TO PROVOKE EFFECTIVE THINKING . . .*

Teach to learn

Consider an idea or topic you are trying to better understand, and create a list of fundamental questions that will guide you to a complete explanation, including motivation, examples, overview, and details, of that subject. With those questions (and their corresponding answers) in hand, prepare a minilecture and consider delivering it to some audience—family, friends, or even a teacher. Ask

them questions to measure how well you understood
and articulated your message.

▶ **Illustration: Question Mark**

Mark is an extremely successful high school mathematics teacher. When we asked him when he really learned
calculus, he said, "When I first taught it. There is no
better way to learn anything than to actually teach it.
When I teach something, I have to confront many fundamental questions: What is the motivation to learn this
topic? What are the basic examples? On what aspects
of this material should I focus? What are the underlying
themes? What ties the ideas together? What is the global
structure? What are the important details? These questions force me to discover the heart of the matter, and
see exactly what I truly understand and what I still need
to work on."

. . . BE YOUR OWN SOCRATES ◀

In the "Fatigues" episode of *Seinfeld*, George has to
address the business executives in the Yankees organization on risk management, but he is unable to
motivate himself to read a book on the subject. After
several funny failed attempts, he enlists the help of an
unsuspecting young protégée, Abby, who looks up
to George as a mentor. Abby is dazzled that George
would take the time to mentor her, and he tells her

that he was once just as much a novice as she is now, one who didn't even know anything about risk management. When she admits to being unfamiliar with the subject, he hornswoggles her into reading the book and explaining its contents to him. By the end of the episode, who do you think learned the basics of risk management?

Is the standard preparation really preparing you? In most mathematics classes, the only opportunity for students to practice the ideas and techniques at hand is through regularly assigned homework. Students often leisurely pursue these exercises at night in their rooms while lying on their beds, listening to their iPods, and text messaging their friends. Somehow, over the course of the evening, the assignment is completed.

But how are the *major* assessments conducted? Through a couple of pressure-packed, timed exams in which students are placed in a sterile classroom, sitting in tiny seats, surrounded by other equally anxious students. While we, the authors, question the true educational value of such academic sprinting, this mode of assessment remains prevalent. So the question is, When do we teach students how to perform well under such time pressure? The answer is *never*. No wonder so many people have "math phobia."

To prepare students effectively, instructors should teach students how to perform under the same conditions that they will face when the major assessment occurs. For example, teachers could give pressure-packed sixty-second in-class exercises in which students are to work fast while the teacher yells at them to work faster. These seemingly harsh episodes actually would give students experience in focusing, not being distracted, and engaging with the material quickly and accurately. When the real tests rolled around, students would not crumble under any intense pressure. As a student, challenge yourself to attempt homework as quickly as possible—consider these questions: How fast can I do this assignment? How much can I get done in thirty minutes even if, at the moment, I can't get it all right? You are now practicing for the big exam, and you can always go back and correct any errors you might have made during that lightning round. So in preparing for anything, ask yourself, "What can I do on a day-to-day basis to help me perform well when it counts?"

Creating questions enlivens your curiosity

A questionable habit. If you want to get more out of what you hear or see, *force* yourself to ask questions—in a lecture, at a meeting, while listening to music, watching TV, or viewing art. People who ask lots of probing questions outperform those who don't engage with the ideas. Constantly generate questions and then ask them—that mind-set will lead to a richer appreciation of the issues.

If you are a teacher or a manager, instead of asking, "Are there any questions?" *assume* there are, and say, "Talk to your neighbor for sixty seconds and write down two questions." Then randomly call on pairs to read their questions. That is, instead of asking *whether* there are questions, tell your listeners that they are to *create* questions—an important habit to develop for lifelong learning and curiosity.

Whether or not you are asked to write down questions, constantly come up with questions on your own. Of course, actually *asking* the questions you create is also an excellent exercise—it allows for further clarity, and it shows the presenter you're genuinely thinking about the material. But even if you would rather not raise those questions, just the act of creating them adds tremendous value. Writing your own test before an exam or quiz is a good idea, but don't wait. Every day put yourself in the position of an evaluator and create your own test for everything you hear, see, or read. Ask yourself, "What would someone ask me in order to determine whether I really understand these ideas?"

Be thought provoking. Getting in the habit of asking questions will transform you into an *active* (rather than passive) listener. This practice forces you to have a different inner life experience, since you will, in fact, be listening more effectively. You know that sometimes when you are supposed to be listening to someone or reading something, your mind starts to wander. All teachers (and parents) know that this happens frequently with students in classes.

It's what goes on inside *your* head that makes all the difference in how well you will convert what you hear into something you learn. Listening is not enough. If you are constantly engaged in asking yourself questions about what you are hearing, you will find that even boring lecturers become a bit more interesting, because much of the interest will be coming from what *you* are generating rather than what the lecturer is offering. When someone else speaks, *you* need to be thought provoking!

Be an official questioner. Every day in each of my classes I (BURGER) randomly select two students who are given the title of "official questioners." These students are assigned the responsibility to pose at least one question during that class. After being the day's official questioner early in the term at Baylor University, one of my students, Carrie, visited me in my office. Just to break the ice, I leaned back in my chair and asked in a lighthearted way, "Did you feel honored to be named one of the first 'official questioners' of the semester?" Much to my surprise, she assumed a serious and pensive tone and confessed that she'd been extremely nervous when I appointed her at the beginning of class. But then, during that class, she felt differently from how she'd felt during other lectures. It was a lecture just like the others, but this time, she said, she was forced to have a higher level of consciousness; she was more alive, more aware of what went on, and more attuned to the subtler content of the discussion. She also admitted that as a result she got more out of that class.

Carrie's role as official questioner made her experience the mental activity that is required in each class by every student who wishes to succeed, understand, and ace the course. She not only asked a question that day, but she became a regular question-poser and added a great deal of value—not only to her own understanding, but also to the class discussions. Carrie actually *changed* how she *learned* in a classroom environment, and how she listened every day of her life. With practice, you can learn to take personal responsibility to understand what is being said as it happens in real time, and to actively construct well-founded questions about what is missing, what is assumed, what might be extended, or what is vague or unclear. If you embrace these habits of mind—forcing yourself to create and ask questions when you are listening to a lecture or anything else—you will find there are at least two effects: one, you will perform better; and, two, you will find the world more engaging.

What's the *real* question?

Sadly, many people spend their entire lives focusing on the wrong questions. They may pursue money, when they really want happiness. They may pursue the respect of people whose favor is really not worthy of being sought. So before you succumb to the temptation to immediately spring to work on the answer, always stop and first ask, "What's the *real* question here?" Often the question that seems obvious may not be the question that leads to effective action.

Personal questions such as "How can I be successful?" or "How can I ace my exam?" or societal questions such as "Why do African Americans underperform on math tests?" are important, but they are not *effective* questions. Effective questions turn your mind in directions that lead to new insights and solutions. They highlight hidden assumptions and indicate directions to take to make progress. So what's wrong with the previous three questions, and how might we fix them?

"How can I be successful?" is vague, and, until you first carefully define "successful," it is unanswerable. You should first ask what success means for you and then pose questions that lead to action. When you ask about success, are you really asking about making money? If so, are you making a hidden assumption?

Is a Wall Street banker who is fabulously wealthy, but unhappy, successful? Is an artist who lives in poverty, never sells a painting, but loves his art, successful? You must define success for yourself. Only then will you be able to ask the right questions about how *you* can be successful. The effective questions you will ask about success will lead you to explore and develop core values, habits, and skills that will make a difference.

Effective questions lead to action and are not vague

"How can I ace my exam?" If you're a student, you are naturally concerned with how you perform on examinations. But, ironically, focusing on the impending test itself is not the best way to improve your performance on it. Suppose in a few months you were going to be asked to do thirty push-ups. You could concentrate on what to eat the day before the push-up competition, and what shirt to wear that's not too tight or too loose, and how to give 110% at the time of the challenge. Or you could slowly, over time, increase the number of push-ups you can do each day between now and then so that it would be no effort to pump out thirty push-ups at test time. "How can I do my best on the exam?" is not the best question to ask in school. Better questions include these: "How can I become more engaged in the course material?" "Could I give a lecture explaining the material?" "Could I write a

detailed outline for this course?" These questions lead to actions that you can take—becoming an active listener, joining a study group, or, even better, tutoring others.

The right questions clarify your understanding and focus your attention on features that matter

"Why do African Americans underperform on math tests?" Billions of dollars and much frustrating effort are spent trying to answer questions such as this. But it's the wrong question. This question draws our attention to the wrong variable, namely, race, rather than the variables that actually impact the performance of *any* student of *any* race. Pertinent variables might include teaching methods, available resources, the amount of constructive help a student receives, the level of encouragement and motivation, study habits and attitudes, time on task, feeling of belonging and confidence during instruction, and the student's history of success or failure. Questions concerning these themes and their relationship to any student's success direct our attention in constructive ways. They point our minds toward features of reality that may have an impact on individual student performance, and that can possibly lead to useful interventions directed not at racially profiled populations, but at underperforming populations that include students of all races and ethnicities.

Effective questions expose the real issue

Seeking the right question forces you to realize that there are at least two kinds of ignorance: cases in which you know the right question but not the answer, and cases in which you don't even know which question to ask.

▶ *A WAY TO PROVOKE EFFECTIVE THINKING . . .*

Improve the question

From a student's point of view, the question "How can I get better grades?" is not the most effective route to higher grades. Questions such as "How can I learn to think better and understand more deeply?" "How can I learn to communicate better?" "How can I increase my curiosity?" are far more constructive. For the questions below that are relevant to you, and more importantly for the ones you will create, craft more focused questions that might lead to a productive conclusion. Try to create questions that expose hidden assumptions, clarify issues, and lead to action.

- "How can I better manage my time?"
- "How can I land that dream job within the next four years?"
- "How can I attract this potential client?"
- "How can I quit a bad habit?"
- "How can I get my students to perform better?"

Apply this exercise whenever you are confronted with a question in your own life—that is, constantly question your own questions.

▶ **Illustration: Traffic**

While stuck (and frustrated) in bumper-to-bumper traffic that is moving at a painfully slow crawl, you wonder (perhaps in more colorful language), "How can this traffic problem be fixed?!?" The answers are easy but not practical: increase the flow by widening the roads or constructing additional highways. But the reality is that unless you're the president or governor, you cannot make either solution happen. Thus your frustration level rises along with your blood pressure. Your question was not a great one. Instead ask, "Given that I will spend an extra forty minutes in traffic, how can I use that time effectively?" Now you're asking a question that is productive. You might consider books on tape to entertain or educate you, or language tapes to improve your Greek, or visits with distant family and friends via Bluetooth.

. . . BE YOUR OWN SOCRATES ◀

The right questions in the classroom. When a teacher gives an assignment, that instructor has the pedagogical responsibility to ask, "What beneficial change will this exercise help foster or develop in my students?"

and afterward, "What permanent lessons have these activities advanced?" If you are a student, it is crucial to ask the corresponding questions: "What beneficial change could this assignment offer me?" "What permanent benefit am I supposed to get out of this exercise?" "Did I get it?" In our experience, the people who ask and act on these questions are more successful than those who don't.

For example, realize that every time you write anything, you can harness that moment as an opportunity to improve your communication and argumentation skills, which can help you literally every day at home, at work, and in the world. Teachers should craft assignments that promote long-term goals such as communicating and thinking more effectively. By asking questions about goals, you are better able to extract the advantages from assignments rather than mindlessly checking them off your to-do list. Remember to always question the questions.

▶ *A WAY TO PROVOKE EFFECTIVE THINKING . . .*

Ask meta-questions

Whether in the classroom, the boardroom, or the living room, asking questions about an assignment or project *before* beginning work in earnest will always lead to a stronger final product. Ask, "What's the goal of this task?" and "What benefit flows from the task?" Keep that benefit in mind as you move forward. A by-product of this exercise is that it often saves time, because it focuses your attention on the core issues and allows you to quickly clear up the initial confusion that always is present at the start of any project or task.

▶ **Illustration: Bear essentials**

A classic joke illustrates the importance of focusing on the right question: Two men are walking in the woods. A ferocious grizzly bear charges at them and they start to run. While running, they shout:

> *Man 1*: We'll never outrun the bear.
> *Man 2*: I don't have to. My only question is "Can I outrun you?"

Man 2 has identified the right question.

. . . BE YOUR OWN SOCRATES ◀

There is nothing so useless as doing efficiently that which should not be done at all.

—Peter Drucker

Teachers often misunderstand their role in enabling their students to learn. It's tempting to view the good teacher's job as chewing up the knowledge into morsels small enough for the students to swallow. But the real goal is for students to develop skills and attitudes that will allow them to independently think through the complications of life and find ways to learn for themselves. So the teacher may be asking the wrong question when he or she asks, "How can I make this difficult material easier for my students?"

Frequently students are told explicitly or implicitly that the goal of school is to make good grades and earn a diploma. Those are not worthy goals of education. What should be the goals of education beyond good grades and a sheepskin? Ideally, the goal of education should be to develop critical thinking and communication skills and other such mind-strengthening abilities. If the teachers, the students, and the broader community are clear about the appropriate goals for education, the daily experience of students changes for the better.

Final thoughts: The art of creating questions and active listening

The right questions can be incredibly powerful tools for understanding and learning. Great questions can lead to insights that will make a difference. You can create great questions using concrete and straightforward techniques—questions that guide you and arouse your curiosity. Questions give us a breath of inspiration and insight; thus we associate the art of questioning with the element Air.

Constantly thinking of questions is a mind-set with tremendous impact. You become more alive and curious, because you are actively engaged while you are listening and living. You become more open to ideas, because you are constantly discovering places where your assumptions are exposed. You take more effective action, because you clarify what needs to be done. Be your own Socrates.

 **Water**

4. Seeing the Flow of Ideas
Look Back, Look Forward

> **To improve the golden moment of opportunity, and catch the good that is within our reach, is the great art of life.**
>
> **—Samuel Johnson**

An illuminated lightbulb is the iconic metaphor for a bright, original idea. But one part of the metaphor is simply wrong—the brightness of a lightbulb occurs in a vacuum, whereas ideas never arise in a void. New ideas today are built on the ideas of yesterday and illuminate the way to the brilliant ideas of tomorrow. Innovators—inventors such as Alexander Graham Bell, artists such as Claude Monet, scientists such as Charles Darwin, writers such as J. K. Rowling, and business leaders such as Steve Jobs—recognize that each new idea extends a line that started in the past and travels through the present into the future. Successful and effective learners and innovators harness the power of the flow of ideas, which suggests the element Water.

There's always more: every advance can be the launchpad to far greater advances yet to be discovered.

An Apple computer built in a garage in the 1970s has evolved into its current state and will soon be unrecognizably more advanced. Solutions to little problems generate solutions to great problems.

History erased. Have you ever sat in a lecture totally lost or read some profound idea in a book and thought to yourself, "How did anyone ever come up with this stuff?!" Great question. Unfortunately origins of ideas are often covered up, giving the impression of magic, spontaneous creation rather than of incremental evolution, which is a far more accurate description.

Every great idea is a *human* idea that evolved from hundreds if not thousands of individuals struggling to make sense of and understand the issue at hand. Thoughtful individuals moved the boundaries of our knowledge forward little by little; often by applying the elements of thinking that we've considered in the previous chapters—understanding deeply, failing, and asking questions. Every wandering step, every misstep, and every dead end provided a new insight that moved those struggling minds along the path of discovery.

▶ *A WAY TO PROVOKE EFFECTIVE THINKING . . .*

Iterate ideas
You don't need an army of thousands of individuals to struggle a thousand years to address a challenge. The

only person who needs to move forward little by little is you. *Engineer your own evolution.* Take a homework assignment, essay, or project that you're facing and quickly *just do it*; that is, tackle the questions, draft the essay, or move forward on the project at a fast-forward speed that will surely generate a work that is, at best, subpar. Now consider that poor effort as your starting point: react to that work and start to improve and iterate. The flow of iteration will lead to a refined final product. Notice how this flowing mind-set perfectly coincides with the elements of failure we introduced earlier.

▶ **Illustration: Rewriting in Ernest**

Ernest Hemingway was interviewed for an article entitled "The Art of Fiction," which appeared in the *Paris Review* in 1956. The interview revealed Hemingway as a person who practiced the technique of incremental progress.

Interviewer: How much rewriting do you do?

Hemingway: It depends. I rewrote the ending of *A Farewell to Arms*, the last page of it, thirty-nine times before I was satisfied.

Interviewer: Was there some technical problem there? What was it that had stumped you?

Hemingway: Getting the words right.

. . . SEE THE FLOW OF IDEAS ◀

To understand *current* ideas through flow, first find easier elements that lead to what you want to understand, and then build bridges from those easier elements to the ideas you wish to master. To generate *new* ideas through flow, first modify an existing idea within its own context and then apply that same idea in different settings. Then you can construct extensions, refinements, and variations.

Understanding current ideas through the flow of ideas

To truly understand a concept, discover how it naturally evolves from simpler thoughts. Recognizing that the present reality is a moment in a continuing evolution makes your understanding fit into a more coherent structure.

Turning the page on calculus. The whole history of mathematics is one long sequence of taking the best ideas of the moment and finding new extensions, variations, and applications. Our lives today are totally different from the lives of people three hundred years ago, mostly owing to scientific and technological innovations that required the insights of calculus. Isaac Newton and Gottfried von Leibniz independently discovered calculus in the last half of the seventeenth century. But a study of the history reveals that mathematicians had thought of all the essential elements of calculus before either Newton or Leibniz came along. Newton himself acknowledged this flowing reality when he wrote, "If I have seen farther than others it is because I have stood on the shoulders of giants." Newton and Leibniz came up with their brilliant insight at essentially the same time because it was not a huge leap from what was already known. All creative people, even ones who are considered geniuses, start as nongeniuses and take baby steps from there.

Calculus truly changed the world; but it didn't change the world on the day it was discovered. During the past three hundred years, calculus has been applied to mechanics, to the motion of the planets, to electricity and magnetism, to fluid flow, to biology, to economics, as well as to countless other areas. Calculus may hold a world's record for how far an idea can be pushed. Leibniz published the first article on calculus in 1684, an essay that was a mere 6 pages long. Newton and Leibniz would surely be astounded to learn that today's introductory calculus textbook contains over 1,300 pages. A calculus textbook introduces two fundamental ideas, and the remaining 1,294 pages consist of examples, variations, and applications—all arising from following the consequences of just two fundamental ideas.

Students might be amazed that their teachers know all 1,300 pages of that enormous tome filled with cryptic symbols. But their teachers don't really know 1,300 independent pages of isolated facts—the teachers see the material differently. They know the meaning of the basic ideas, and they know how one idea leads to another. Students who duplicate that perspective grasp the ideas of any subject better than those students who view each new week as an entirely new intellectual mountain to climb. As you are learning a topic, ask yourself what previous knowledge and what strategy of extending previous ideas make the new idea clear, intuitive, and a natural extension.

Every subject is an ongoing journey of discovery and development. It is not just a laundry list of disconnected topic, topic, topic, but a flow of ideas that build upon each other. When we see and understand that these ideas are connected, they become more interesting, more memorable, and more meaningful. Remember: If you can't get 100% on your last test (actual or metaphorical), then you're not ready for your next exam.

▶ *A WAY TO PROVOKE EFFECTIVE THINKING . . .*

Think back

Whenever you face an issue—whether an area of study or a decision about a future path—consider what came before. Wonder how the issue at hand landed in front of you. Ask where and what it was yesterday, a month ago, a year ago, and so forth. Everything, everyone has a history and evolves. Acknowledging that reality will allow you to generate new insights as well as create fruitful directions in which to move forward.

▶ **Illustration: Penning the prequel**

Juan finished reading a novel and was reflecting on it. That story took place during the Cold War. He decided to consider what had happened before the Cold War heated up. That is, before the story unfolded in the pages of the book, where were those characters? What were their histories? How did those individuals evolve into the characters that come to life on the page? His answers helped him to explain certain dynamics and allowed him to better understand the actions and story lines. Of course, the bookend question "What comes next?" (that is, "What transpired beyond the end of the book itself?") is the next natural issue to contemplate.

. . . SEE THE FLOW OF IDEAS ◀

Guessing what's next anchors what's there. To better
master a subject, after you have been introduced to a
new concept, look beyond the new concept and just
guess what you think will come next—in a text or in
a lecture or in any presentation. Even if your con-
jecture is not right, it's still important. Being wrong
allows you to better realize what is truly there, and
offers insights as to how the ideas might actually fit
together.

A few years ago, I (BURGER) sat in on an art history class with a couple of undergraduate students
whose primary field of interest was mathematics. We
never took notes and didn't have a course syllabus.
During our walk to the lecture hall each class day,
we got in the habit of guessing—just based on what
we remembered from the previous class—what was
to be the topic of the day's lecture. These discussions
were a profound way to make the whole class more
meaningful and more memorable. They caused us to
thoughtfully review what had been discussed in the
class before and also helped us to consciously frame
the progression of artistic ideas, and to think of the
subject as a whole rather than as a collection of disconnected artistic periods.

Even when our guesses were completely off, they
still helped us to view the previous material more
fully by thinking how the earlier material might have
looked in the middle of a stream of progress rather
than in isolation. Learning from mistaken guesses

let us see differences between what we expected and what actually arose, and thus changed our view of the issues. The whole subject became an interconnected web of ideas. As an aside, with just these conversations on the way to class as well as active listening during lectures—but without reading the text, taking notes, or even attending the weekly conference sections—we actually passed the exams!

A look back makes earlier material easier. Once you understand a more advanced topic, look back to see what brought you to where you are. That process will improve your understanding both of the earlier work and of the more advanced work. The earlier material will become easier, clearer, and more meaningful because you will see its significance through the later work that came from it. The more advanced work will also be easier since you will now see how it grew from the seeds that existed in the earlier work. We have seen that the most successful people regularly undertake this important reflective exercise. Remember trumpet virtuoso Tony Plog's challenge of playing a simple passage and making it sing.

One small step. One of the most heartening realities of human thought is that all the new ideas we have are, in fact, only tiny variations of what has been thought before. If we look back on the history of inventions or the evolution of ideas, it may appear that there were moments of lightning-strike inspiration that led in totally new directions. But, as we saw with the birth of calculus, essentially every important brilliant idea can easily be seen to be the result of someone's understanding what was already known and taking a small step to reveal the next idea—another variation on understanding simple things deeply.

The difference between those who have great insights and those who don't is that the first group actually take those baby steps. Students who embrace the mind-set that better ideas are literally right next door and that "one more small step will get me there" outperform those who believe that only the great minds make great progress. Taking these little steps can have tremendous implications for everything from writing essays and performing lab experiments to launching the next Internet craze.

Art. The progression of artistic periods over the centuries presents a dramatic picture of the evolution of aesthetic norms as reactions to the current artistic status quo. The impressionist movement was several steps away from the representational art that preceded it. It broke with the conventional wisdom that a painting should look like what we would describe as a photograph. Instead, impressionist painters—having mastered the established stylistic techniques of the day—aimed to take a step forward by creating the essence of a scene without offering a crystal-clear picture of it, thus inviting the viewer to actively engage with and interpret the works.

While today we look upon these paintings as masterpieces, when they were first shown in the salons of France, the public was appalled and actually offended. Those viewers didn't know how to interpret the revolutionary style, and so they simply panned the work. In fact one reviewer, in his scathing critique, wrote that these works were not even art, but rather merely "impressions" of the images depicted. What was then an insulting slur now denotes one of the most important artistic periods.

In thinking about the future, we must be conscious of the reality that the novelties that appear strange to us today will be familiar, natural, and perhaps even beautiful to the next generation, and possibly even to us in the future. One of the challenges of life is to be open-minded about new ideas and new possibilities. It was difficult to accept impressionism when art was assumed to be a method of representing how the world actually looks. Each of us has the challenge of seeing the impressionism of our time as a valid, interesting, and important window into the world of tomorrow.

Creating new ideas from old ones

When you learn a new concept or master a skill, think about what extensions, variations, and applications are possible. It's natural to think of the moment when you've solved a problem or mastered a new idea as a time to party and rest on your laurels—as if you've arrived at the final chapter of some great story. In fact, a bed of laurels will never offer a satisfying rest, and a new idea or solution should always be viewed as a *beginning*. Effective students and creative innovators regularly strive to uncover the unintended consequences of a lesson learned or a new idea.

The time to work on a problem is after you've solved it.

—R. H. Bing

An illuminating illustration. Thomas Edison was supremely successful at inventing product after product, exploiting the maxim that every new idea has utility beyond its original intent, for he wrote, "I start where the last man left off." More poignantly he noted that "many of life's failures are people who did not realize how close they were to success when they gave up."

The lightbulb solved an extremely important problem, providing us with illumination at any time to perform functions that had previously required daylight.

But that solution was only a tiny tip of a monumental iceberg. Pushing the idea of the lightbulb led to otherwise unforeseen frontiers including movies, televisions, computers, copy machines, fiber optics, medical procedures, tanning beds, and even heat sources at buffets. Before the invention of the lightbulb, people could not imagine the incredibly rich and varied developments that would stem from it, but in fact every idea, though it may seem to solve just one isolated problem, is only the tiny tip of its own monumental iceberg.

> **I begin with an idea and then it becomes something else.**
> **—Pablo Picasso**

Dial M for more. Think of the number of steps of improvement that started with Alexander Graham Bell's telephone. You've seen old movies in which the single rotary telephone in a large mansion sat on a table in the entryway. Later, telephone extensions allowed phones to be placed in different rooms; then touch-tone phones; then cordless phones; then large, brick-like cellular phones; then pocket-sized cell phones with cameras; then smartphones with Internet access and video. And surely no one believes that the iPhone is the end of the line. Each of these steps required thinking of the current pinnacle of development of an idea and asking, "How could that current solution be refined to solve the problem it solved even better?"

It is not only technological ideas that are developed and modified. Look at artistic developments or philosophical or societal or religious ideas. You might argue that in those realms new developments may not always be improvements; however, you must agree that evolving ideas have transformed all these areas. No religion today would imprison Galileo—as the Catholic Church did in 1633—for asserting that Earth moves around the sun. The artistic variety of today could not have been dreamed of centuries ago. Movies, literature, and cultural expression all develop by taking the best of one generation and going beyond in the next.

A weed is a plant whose virtue has not yet been discovered.

—Ralph Waldo Emerson

▶ *A WAY TO PROVOKE EFFECTIVE THINKING . . .*

Extend ideas

Take a good idea from any arena—work, society, or personal life. It need not be an idea you yourself originated. Now engage with that idea and extend it. The key is not to wonder *whether* the idea has extensions; it does. Your challenge is to find them.

▶ **Illustration: Going once, going twice, sold**

In 1995 Pierre Omidyar was considering the effectiveness of auctions and how well they have worked for centuries. He wondered how he could extend that method of sales to include millions of bidders. He turned to the Internet and voilà! eBay was born.

. . . SEE THE FLOW OF IDEAS ◀

The best can get even better. Just as our own understanding can be deeper and richer than it currently is—no matter where it is in its evolution—an important perspective of successful thinking is that the best can be improved. In fact, starting with what is currently the best is often the ideal place to expect great improvements. We limit ourselves when we think that success is an end.

Sometimes getting to the current highest level of perfection was so difficult or so satisfying that we can't imagine further heights. Often the solution to a difficult problem comes from a struggled focus on the issue. Having been in the trenches working on that issue, you naturally feel like a climber reaching the summit after arduous toil. You have arrived. You feel that you are just barely standing on a precarious perch, and your memories are filled with the details and the triumphs of the climb. But a newcomer, who has that summit as his or her initial position, has a different vantage point. The newcomer did not experience the toil, did not live through the trials and failures and hard-won small steps. The young person or the person new to the field sees that issue in its solved condition as just the way the world is.

Babies born today enter a world replete with computers, the Internet, smartphones, text messaging, jet planes, and hundreds of cable TV channels. Children who hear about the olden days when phones were attached to walls by wires are learning about a foreign, quaint, antiquated world. Children or newcomers start where we are now and, without the burden or bias of history, proceed forward. So one of the challenges for us all is to see—with fresh eyes—the current world for what it is now. Knowing the history is certainly helpful, but not if we tend to see current solutions as summits. We must get in the habit of seeing each advance as putting us on the *lower* slope of a much *higher* peak that has yet to be scaled.

Ransom Olds, the father of the Oldsmobile, could not produce his "horseless carriages" fast enough. In 1901 he had an idea to speed up the manufacturing process—instead of building one car at a time, he created the *assembly line*. The acceleration in production was unheard-of—from an output of 425 automobiles in 1901 to an impressive 2,500 cars the following year.

While other competitors were in awe of this incredible volume, Henry Ford dared to ask, "Can we do even better?" He was, in fact, able to improve upon Olds's clever idea by introducing conveyor belts to the assembly line. As a result, Ford's production went through the (sun)roof. Instead of taking a day and a half to manufacture a Model T, as in the past, he was now able to spit them out at a rate of one car every ninety minutes. The moral of the story is that good progress is often the herald of great progress.

The same is true of learning new and increasingly difficult concepts or mastering skills at increasingly higher levels. You may have to struggle to finally master an idea or a skill. Having toiled to get that far, you may think that it would be impossible to go yet further, or you may just feel worn out. But after you have reached one level, that is where you start. That is the platform from which you can proceed even further—whether that starting point is a high grade, a professional accomplishment, or a profound insight; go for it!

▶ *A WAY TO PROVOKE EFFECTIVE THINKING . . .*

Once you have it, see if you can improve it
Take an essay you've written or a solution to an issue and create a different, better one. *Assume* there is a mistake

or omission or missed opportunity in your work—there always is! Now find it (yet another example of the insights we can gain by failing). This activity is much more challenging than it might at first appear. We are biased and limited by what we already know—especially since we know it works. However, moving beyond that bias can lead to new answers that, in turn, can lead to new insights and more effective solutions. People who make this evolutionary iteration a standard practice are far more successful in their education and in life than those who see an answer as an end.

▶ **Illustration: A better Shanice**

Shanice decided to apply this exercise to herself. She considered her best personal assets and wondered how to make them far better still. She plays the cello and her sight-reading is amazing, so she considered improving that skill. She knits beautiful scarves using complicated lace patterns, so she considered improving that talent. She finally decided to focus on her passion for rugby and worked to improve her already strong passing abilities. Working on strengths can have unexpected payoffs, including, paradoxically, remedying weaknesses. In this case, improving her passing involved communicating more effectively with her teammates, which thus led Shanice to improve her previously weak communication skills both on and off the field. Working on strengths is a feature of successful thinking and learning that takes everyone—including Shanice—to new heights.

. . . SEE THE FLOW OF IDEAS ◄

Making it practical. Human beings do not instantly see far. Our field of intellectual vision is limited to a few steps from where we are now. We must acknowledge that however far we do see, our vision extends merely to a horizon beyond which a far bigger world will become visible. How can we start the process of exploring where new ideas can lead us? Ask, "What's next?" Explore the connective, "If this, then that." Follow the hypothetical results of the idea. And when you have arrived at the next step, let it settle as the new reality and only then think, "What now?" By doing so, you will move from thinking of a subject as a student to thinking about the issues as a practitioner. You will be thinking in a different way—which, of course, is the entire point.

To be sure, not every sequence of consequences that we imagine will actually come to pass or lead to fertile new ground, but exploring those consequences several steps forward can have great value. Following that flow can highlight some fallacies in seemingly sound schemes. For example, suppose you wanted to improve air travel by making it safer. Following the possible consequences of improved airline safety may lead to a surprising conclusion. Improved airline safety could actually result in *more* total deaths, because if the increased safety leads to higher costs for flying, then more people might be forced to drive, which is a far more fatal way to travel.

To envision the future, look back and put yourself in the mind-set of the past. For example, think about how difficult it would have been thirty years ago to envision the Internet. Ask yourself, "What object or idea of tomorrow would be as unimaginable today as the World Wide Web was in 1980?" For example, we can imagine Google Glasses™ that will bring the Internet to your eyewear, in which the interface is accomplished by thoughts alone. You may think this vision is pure fantasy, but consider how impossible smartphones (without cords) would have seemed in the 1970s—it was the science fiction of its time. Think one step back to imagine one step forward.

Nothing is easier than seeing the ridiculous biases of the past or the ridiculous biases that other people hold. But nothing is harder than seeing the ridiculous biases that we accept ourselves. By extrapolating the flow of future ideas, we can identify invisible problems today.

▶ *A WAY TO PROVOKE EFFECTIVE THINKING . . .*

Ask: What were they thinking?

What beliefs, cultural habits, opinions, or actions that are completely accepted today will be viewed as ridiculous by our grandchildren? What are some possible candidates? Centuries ago, perfectly respectable people viewed slavery as a natural and moral practice. What practices that we accept as fine today will be condemned as offensive in the future?

▶ **Illustration: The permanent "F"**

Today it is unacceptable to tell racial or ethnic jokes. These jokes are considered demeaning and reflective of prejudice. We are now sensitive to groups that might be insulted or debased in some way. This view is obvious to most cultured individuals. Now let's consider our current educational system. Every semester at every school in the country, report cards define significant numbers of the students as inferior. They are individually singled out and told, "You are not smart enough; you are not industrious enough; you are inadequate; you are inferior." As a cultural norm, we are careful not to hurt people's feelings with slurs on their ethnic backgrounds or religious practices, yet we consider it perfectly acceptable to tell people explicitly, through their failing grades, that they are inferior. There are alternatives. Perhaps, in the future, failing grades would not be recorded at all—only the knowledge and skills that a student actually mastered would make it onto his or her transcript. Does it make sense to record on the student's permanent record the fact that he or she did not succeed in Bio 101 in a particular semester? Perhaps in the future we will not punish students for not "getting it" the first time.

. . . SEE THE FLOW OF IDEAS ◀

You might disagree that reporting a student's bad grade is an immoral act, and we, the authors, are not suggesting that this practice will necessarily be viewed any differently later. But *any* example of a practice that is accepted today but will be viewed as immoral in the future *must* be a custom that we now view as perfectly fine. Only in the future will that cultural norm be viewed from a different angle and deemed unacceptable.

The moral here is that we all hold biases, and viewing our culture's attitudes as evolving perspectives can help us uncover those biases. Some of our strongly held beliefs are based on plausible notions that we either read or heard, but many of our most firmly held convictions are not based on concrete, verifiable fact or proof. It is impossible to avoid bias—it infuses itself through our upbringing, our values, our society, and our community. The first real action item for all of us is to acknowledge (unabashedly) that we are all prejudiced.

This self-conscious understanding of underlying bias is an important step if we are to begin to move forward.

Final thoughts: "Under construction" is the norm

Many people believe that the ideal state of the world is one in which everything is finished and perfect. In fact, a little arithmetic shows that that perspective is simply wrong. For example, New York City is the home of approximately 200 skyscrapers. A building lasts perhaps 40 years before it needs a major renovation or replacement. It requires perhaps 4 years with construction crews conspicuously present to renovate a skyscraper. So that means that on average 5 (200 ÷ 40) skyscrapers per year will start a major overhaul, so possibly 20 (4 × 5) skyscrapers on average are under major construction each year in New York City, adding to the chaos and commotion for which the city is famous. It is more realistic and healthier to view our world as one in which construction is always under way—everything is a work-in-progress.

By analogy, your life has many major features— family, friends, education, professional situations, possessions, and more. Each of these elements is in flux. So you should not expect the "normal" state of affairs to be one in which everything is finished, perfect, and performing well. In reality, the normal state is one in which some features of life and learning are problematic and need attention. Acknowledge that reality and try to identify opportunities for improvement and growth. Expect and embrace change, and use the reality and perspective of the flow of ideas to help you both to understand the world and to create new worlds to come.

The right dream. You may dream of creating that one new idea that will solve lots of problems (and lead to fame and fortune). But the better dream is to see yourself standing on what seems to be the summit and climbing higher by taking one small step after another. That modest habit of effective thinking will help you accomplish things you never dreamed possible.

 **The Quintessential Element**

5. Engaging Change
Transform Yourself

> I shall be telling this with a sigh
> Somewhere ages and ages hence:
> Two roads diverged in a wood, and I—
> I took the one less traveled by,
> And that has made all the difference.
>
> —From "The Road Not Taken" by Robert Frost

The fifth element of effective learning and thinking is the simplest and most difficult, the most important and most dispensable. If this chapter doesn't resonate with you, just skip it. In some sense, the four preceding elements of effective thinking and learning paint the entire picture.

Each of the preceding four techniques has the goal of changing you into someone who thinks and learns better. In ancient Greek philosophy, the quintessential element was the unchanging material from which the extraterrestrial realm was made. Here the unchanging fifth element is, ironically, change itself. Change is really the goal of the whole story. Through our experience with hundreds of thousands of students, teachers, professionals, business leaders, and lifelong learners, we know that if you follow the lessons in this book, you *will* learn and understand at a deeper level; you *will* think of creative ideas; and you *will* be successful throughout life. The quintessential element is really about the "if you follow the lessons" part of the previous sentence. This chapter is about what is involved in transforming yourself into a more effective learner and thinker.

An ancient Zen dictum states that "the reason happiness is so hard is because it's so easy." Although we don't claim to exactly understand that statement, it does convey an impression that seems apt here. In one sense there is nothing difficult about adopting effective strategies of learning and thinking. You simply need to shrug off perhaps a lifetime's habit of accepting a relatively superficial level of understanding and start understanding more deeply. You simply need to let go of the constraining forces in your life and let yourself fail on the road to success. You simply need to question all the issues you have taken for granted all those years. You simply need to see every aspect of your world as an ever-evolving stream of insights and ideas. You simply need to change. Of course, in reality, change seems hard—not simple. However, like the way to happiness, the path to change is not through greater willpower and harder work, but rather through thinking differently.

The first four elements of effective thinking do the heavy lifting. They invite you to understand fundamental ideas, to look for essential elements, and to extend what you already know. They suggest pointed questions for you to pose to yourself and others that cause you to think of new ideas, and they point out the value of failure and errors on the road to success.

Those four elements are like the (correct) instructions in a diet book: if you eat this and that and don't eat these things, and you exercise in this way, then you will lose weight. But often the real problem is following the instructions. This quintessential element speaks to the challenge of becoming a person who embraces the lessons.

The fifth element is a meta-lesson. It recommends that you adopt the habit of constructive change. Don't be afraid to change any part of yourself—you'll still be there, only better. Our colleague, Bill Guy, told us a story about an administrator who wanted to change a school. One year this headmaster decided to try to improve the instruction by having experts on teaching talk to the faculty members every month. After six months, the headmaster noticed that one of the teachers was not attending the sessions, so he called him in and asked, "Why haven't you been attending the required seminars on how to teach better?" To which the teacher replied, "There's no need for me to attend. I already know how to teach better than I do."

The first four elements enable you to think better than you do; learn better than you do; and be more creative than you are. The fifth element recommends that you actually do it. *Just do it*. Adopt the habit of improvement, whether using our four elements or by any other methods that you find. If the ability to change is part of who you are, then you are liberated from worry about weaknesses or defects, because you can adapt and improve whenever you like.

Definition of insanity: Doing the same thing
  and expecting a different outcome

And now for something completely different. Grab a piece of paper and a pencil. Close your eyes tightly and write the sentence "I am writing as neatly as I can and any mistake I make is unintentional." Now open your eyes and look at what you've written . . . it's not perfect. Now repeat the exercise but this time with your eyes open. Your result will (hopefully) be much better. Writing with your eyes open is a *different* (and easier) task than writing with your eyes closed.

There is a subtle perspective about improvement and about better performance that can alter how you approach the task of changing yourself. Namely, people who perform better can be viewed as actually doing a different task, rather than doing the same task better.

If you play tennis, go to a court and have someone hit you a tennis ball. First, close your eyes and hit it back. Next, have your partner hit you a ball and watch it intently while you swing until it hits your racket. In both cases you're trying to hit the tennis ball, but hitting it with your eyes open is a different task from hitting it with your eyes closed. When great players play tennis, they watch the ball better than a beginner does. They are doing the easier task of hitting the ball while watching it, rather than the more difficult task of hitting the ball by estimating its future location based solely on where it was at the moment it flew over the net.

When plug-and-chug physics students apply formulas with no sense of what they mean or why they are true, those students are doing a difficult task— doing physics with their eyes closed. Students who understand the ideas behind the formulas are doing a different task. They are working with their eyes open. The better students are doing an easier task. Understanding the meaning and reasoning behind the formulas sometimes strikes students as an unnecessary and diversionary step. In reality understanding leads directly to easier future work and better results.

When average students of history sit down to study for a test on the Second World War, they may be faced with memorizing facts such as lists of countries that were allied with each other. The country names may be just words. The groupings may seem arbitrary. But if those students learned what led to that moment, if they saw the maps, if they understood the transportation and communication methods of the time, if they saw that moment as part of a larger story of the flow of human relationships that started before the war's onset and continued afterward, then that moment of conflict would make far more sense.

You may believe that such a recommendation is ridiculous, because it means memorizing far *more* historical facts rather than the original smaller list of historical events of World War II. However, our point is that learning the flow of history—or any subject— makes each part far more stable and meaningful. Ironically, memorizing a smaller number of isolated facts is harder. Suppose you had to memorize the following list of words:

HORSE ORDER BECAUSE EASY IN WE BEFORE SENTENCE A DID LOGICAL IS

Wouldn't it be easier and faster to memorize the following *longer* list of words?

THIS SENTENCE IS EASY TO REMEMBER BECAUSE THE WORDS APPEAR IN A LOGICAL ORDER; THAT IS, WE DID NOT PUT THE CART BEFORE THE HORSE.

The answer is, yes; because the surrounding context gives meaning to the otherwise meaningless, discrete words.

Individuals who are more successful at anything are performing their task with their eyes open; that is, the activity they are doing is different from the activity that less successful people are undertaking. Often people describe the distinction between the skilled practitioner and the less skilled practitioner by saying that the skilled person is better at the task. But a more useful and accurate perspective is that the skilled practitioner is doing a fundamentally different task—one that you could master as well.

> **In a chronically leaking boat, energy devoted to changing vessels is more productive than energy devoted to patching leaks.**
>
> **—Warren Buffett**

To become more skillful and successful, you might think in terms of altering *what* you do, rather than thinking in terms of *how well* you do it. Instead of thinking, "Do it better," think, "Do it differently." If you want to learn a subject, instead of memorizing rules and facts, concentrate on truly understanding the fundamentals deeply. If you want to think of new ideas, don't sit and wait for inspiration. Instead, apply strategies of transformative thinking such as making mistakes, asking questions, and following the flow of ideas.

▶ *A WAY TO PROVOKE EFFECTIVE THINKING . . .*

Expert change

If you're learning something, solving a problem, or developing a skill, imagine in detail what a more skilled practitioner does, or what added knowledge, understanding, and previous experience the expert would bring to the task. In other words, describe the *different* task that an *expert* would be doing compared to what you are currently doing in undertaking your task. Instead of thinking that you are going to be doing something that is harder—requiring more concentration and more effort—think in terms of what kind of knowledge or skill or strategy would make the task an easier one.

▶ Illustration: The pianist

Imagine practicing a piano piece. An expert memorizes the music and thus can look at the keyboard while performing those long jumps. That may be an easier task than reading the music while attempting to strike the correct keys. At a more subtle level, the accomplished musician understands the chord structure and hears each voice of the music, so the expert is doing a different task from that of the person who is merely remembering what keys to press.

. . . ENGAGE CHANGE ◀

The "dumb" student. Everyone is different. Some people are born with bodies that are bigger or smaller, more muscular or more flexible. Not every person is capable of being a world-class marathon runner, no matter what effort he or she might expend on that goal. And not every person is capable of becoming the world's greatest theoretical physicist. But what is most impressive is the distance between what people *could* potentially achieve and what they *do* actually achieve.

Remember Mary? She was the student who thought she couldn't do math, but by making mistakes and facing questions that allowed her to follow where those errors led, she was able to think of a creative and original answer to a challenging question about infinity. The point of her story is that vast potential lurks in us all. Using techniques of thinking that can be practiced and mastered, Mary succeeded wildly and so can you. Are there limits to how far a given individual can go? Yes, but those boundaries are far, far beyond what people generally accept as their own limits.

We could claim that every person is equally capable of everything, and while that assertion might sell books, it is not reality. However, the reality is that you personally can learn far more and be far more creative and successful than you are today.

You can do it

For effective thinking, differences in native ability are dwarfed by habits and methods. Those individuals who may appear to be the brightest in the sense of catching on to things immediately and being able to deal with complexity without getting confused are rarely the most productive, imaginative, or effective.

Some very bright people can keep amazingly complicated things straight, but they may fail to try new perspectives and new ideas. You might want to describe these people as unimaginative, but as you have seen in this book, being imaginative is not an inborn quality. Coming up with new ideas requires the habit of employing thinking techniques that generate new ideas. Being imaginative is a learnable skill, not an inborn characteristic like having blue eyes. The secret to solving problems and coming up with new ideas is not to find different parents, but to use different strategies of transformative thinking.

Hours 1 through 9,999. You have probably heard of the "10,000-hour rule," which encapsulates the idea that a person needs 10,000 hours of practice to become world-class at anything, from art to music to sports to zoology. This book is about what to do during hours 1 through 9,999. The magic of the 10,000-hour rule does not happen at the 10,000th hour. The magic is an accumulated flow of incremental progress in which the journey forward comes from attaining deeper understanding, making mistakes and learning from them, asking questions, and seeing the evolution of ideas. All mastery is actually a continuum.

Einstein moves on. In 1979, the Institute for Advanced Study in Princeton, New Jersey, held the Einstein Centennial Symposium in honor of the one hundredth anniversary of Albert Einstein's birth. One of the speakers told a story about being a young assistant to Einstein. He said that during the job interview with Einstein, he admitted that he did not know much about relativity, to which Einstein replied, "That's okay. I already know about relativity." The speaker's descriptions of working with Einstein were colorful and amusing, but one anecdote was especially pertinent to transformative thinking.

Einstein was a genius. But the speaker described an incident that may illuminate Einstein's success in a way that other descriptions of his brilliance do not. Einstein and his assistant had been working for months on a particular problem. Einstein had a strategy in mind for solving the problem and persistently tried to pursue it. One day, his assistant received a letter that contained the work of some other physicists who had shown that the approach Einstein was taking could not work. The assistant had to deliver the bad news to Einstein. He explained to Einstein the reason that the approach could not work, knowing that many months of hard effort had been wasted on a futile pursuit. Einstein listened with an open mind and understood the reasoning. The very next day, Einstein had taken a totally different tack on the issue that exposed a new perspective and completely solved the problem. Einstein was brilliant. But he was also willing to change in the face of compelling evidence.

Messing things up. Often the most profound advances you can make in your life come through experiences that challenge the life you have. The image of building a life from solid success to solid success is a wonderful dream, but it is only a fantasy. Instead, you must let old ideas crumble in the face of challenges in order to build yet better structures.

Don't mute voices that challenge your beliefs. Listen for whispers of doubt and turn those doubts into helpful and positive tests of assumptions, ideas, and theories. Doubts are strengths when you use them effectively. Our political theatrics in debates and on cable news programs promote an unproductive attitude that doubt is a sign of weakness, when in reality doubt is a badge of strength. In watching political pundits yell at each other on TV, never once have we heard one respond to the other with "That's a better idea, I'm going to change my mind." The unchangeable mind is a closed mind. The result in politics is a calcified lack of innovation and flexibility—gridlock. Doubt can be unsettling, but it does not have to be. You can turn doubt into a comfortable and insightful guide along the road to true change.

If you are open to new ideas, and you allow yourself to follow your changing opinions and passions, they will lead you in directions you did not originally expect to go. In college, huge numbers of students begin to prepare for a career in medicine or law, but only because they are not aware of alternatives. No matter what your stage in life, you are going to develop strengths you do not yet have, and when you do, opportunities will open to you that you have not yet dreamed of.

Holiday at Big Lake. R. L. Moore was one of the most famous mathematics teachers in the mid-twentieth century. He conducted his classes in a very peculiar, but effective, way. He never lectured. Instead, he posed difficult questions, and his students were required to answer them independently without any outside help. In class, Professor Moore started with the student he considered the least able and asked, "Mr. ——, can you answer the next question?" If that student could not answer the question, Professor Moore posed the same question to the next weakest student, and so on, until he found a student who claimed to be able to answer the question. That student would go to the blackboard and present his or her solution. If the other students found no flaw in the answer, then Professor Moore would simply move on to the next question.

Sam Y. was a student in one of Moore's mathematics courses and found himself branded with the dubious distinction of being considered the weakest student in the class. He had never answered a question correctly during the entire fall semester. At that time, the first semester did not end until several weeks after the winter break. During that winter vacation, Sam went with his parents to Big Lake, Texas. His only chance to pass this class was to somehow find a way to answer some of those difficult questions. He isolated himself in his room and thought. He returned to the first questions of the semester. As he looked back at the beginning of the term, the work began to make sense. He saw why the first theorems were true. He built up from the ground floor and, question by question, solidly constructed answers for himself that taught him the material in a deep and meaningful way. He eventually found himself tackling the questions that had not yet been discussed in class.

On the first day back from vacation, Professor Moore turned, as always, to Sam and asked, "Mr. Y., can you answer Question 26?" With a feeling of pride, Sam replied, "Yes, sir, I can." And he could. To the surprise of the other students in the class, he presented his correct solution to Question 26. Professor Moore, however, was not surprised. He had deliberately given his students the challenges that encouraged them to personally find out how to become a quintessential student—how to understand ideas deeply, how to question, how to fail on the road to success, and how to see the flow of ideas. When Sam sat down, Professor Moore asked, "Mr. Y., can you solve Question 27?" "Yes, sir, I can." was his answer. For the remaining two weeks of the term, Sam presented his correct solutions to all the remaining questions. At Big Lake, Mr. Y. had become a quintessential student. He went on to earn a PhD in mathematics, and Dr. Y. had a long and successful career as a professor of mathematics at a major university.

Not every teacher establishes a classroom environment in which student success directly corresponds to becoming an effective learner and innovator. But regardless of any teacher's skills, students can focus on the goal of developing the lifelong habits that will change them forever.

Final thoughts: Becoming the quintessential you

The story of our dear friend Lee provides a final illustration of the transformative effect of real change. Lee decided she wanted to get in better shape. Instead of grasping at the quick, but ineffective, fix of some "miracle" fad diet, Lee made a slight change in how she viewed herself and how she behaved. She began to eat healthful foods and to climb the stairs instead of riding the elevator. Lee became a different person. Consequently, fourteen months later she had lost a total of eighty pounds and today remains fit and healthy. She does not spend her life fighting herself to behave differently from how she would prefer to eat and act. Instead, she now is a person for whom healthful eating and appropriate exercise are natural, easy parts of everyday life. Her strong physical condition is an inevitable consequence of the habits she adopted; moreover, any able-bodied individual who embraces those same habits will become just as fit.

Similarly, if you adopt the elements of thinking suggested in this book and make those habits part of who you are, you *will* develop mental strength and capacity, and you *will* become a more effective and creative thinker. Moreover, applying these elements to yourself leads you to clarify the core of your own self-definition—including your values, morals, ethics, and beliefs. Descartes's *cogito ergo sum* observes that thinking confirms your very existence. Embracing the elements of effective thinking will inevitably lead you to your quintessential self.

When the American Founding Fathers imagined a democracy that would reflect the will of the people, the people they envisioned were thoughtful, independent-thinking citizens who would understand the issues of their day and would turn their own clear wisdom to making sound decisions for the benefit of society. Surely more than ever, the world needs thoughtful voices—voices that can ignore the bombast and heat of shallow excitement and focus instead on thinking calmly and sensibly about long-term goals and consequences. These elements of effective thinking will help you to become a quintessential citizen of the world—contributing personally and professionally, locally and globally.

Whether in school or out, whether young or old, you can choose to be a person who sees boundless opportunities, who enjoys the lifelong process of personal growth and discovery, and who meets challenges and obstacles with innovation and imagination.

Strive for rock-solid understanding (*Earth*).

Fail and learn from those missteps (*Fire*).

Constantly create and ask challenging questions (*Air*).

Consciously consider the flow of ideas (*Water*).

And, of course, remember that learning is a lifelong journey; thus each of us remains a work-in-progress—always evolving, ever changing—and that's *Quintessential* living.

 **Summary**

A Way to Provoke Effective Thinking
A Brief Review

 Earth

1. Grounding your thinking: Understand deeply

- Understand simple things deeply
- Clear the clutter—seek the essential
- See what's there
- See what's missing

Master the basics. Consider a skill you want to improve or a subject area that you wish to understand better. Spend five minutes writing down specific components of the skill or subject area that are basic to that theme. Pick one of the items on your list, and spend thirty minutes actively improving your mastery of it. See how working deeply on the basics makes it possible for you to hone your skill or deepen your knowledge at the higher levels you are trying to attain. Apply this exercise at all scales to other things you think you know or would like to know. (See *p. 18.*)

Ask: What do you know? Do you or don't you truly know the basics? Consider a subject you think you know or a subject you are trying to master. Open up a blank document on your computer. Without referring to any outside sources, write a detailed outline of the fundamentals of the subject. Can you write a coherent, accurate, and comprehensive description of the foundations of the subject, or does your knowledge have gaps? Do you struggle to think of core examples? Do you fail to see the overall big picture that puts the pieces together? When you discover weaknesses in your own understanding of the basics, take action. Methodically, slowly, and thoroughly learn the fundamentals. Repeat this exercise regularly as you learn more advanced aspects of the subject. Every return to the basics will deepen your understanding of the entire subject. (See *p. 21.*)

Sweat the small stuff. Consider some complex issue in your studies or life. Instead of tackling it in its entirety, find one small element of it and solve that part completely. Understand the subissue and its solution backwards and forwards. Understand all its connections and implications. Consider this small piece from many points of view and in great detail. Choose a subproblem small enough that you can give it this level of attention. Only later should you consider how your efforts could help solve the larger issue. (See *p. 25*.)

Uncover one essential. Consider a subject you wish to understand, and clear the clutter until you have isolated one essential ingredient. Each complicated issue has several possible core ideas. You are not seeking "the" essential idea; you are seeking just one—consider a subject and pare it down to one essential theme. In fact, you might perform this exercise on yourself. What do you view as essential elements of you? Isolating those elements can give a great deal of focus to life decisions. (See *p. 30*.)

Say it like you see it. Homework assignments, tests, and job-related assessments ask you what you know. Unfortunately, partial credit or social pressure often encourages you to pretend to know a bit more than you actually do. So in the privacy of your own room look at assignments or possible test questions and write down the weaknesses as well as the strengths of what you know and don't know. Deliberately avoid glossing over any gaps or vagueness. Instead boldly assert what is tepid or missing in your understanding. Then take action. Identifying and admitting your own uncertainties is an enormous step toward solid understanding. (See *p. 35*.)

Try on alternatives and size up the fit. Temporarily embrace some opinion that is counter to what you hold. Try not to be judgmental. Don't resist the alternative views. You are not committing to any change. This exercise has the goal of understanding alternatives more realistically. As a result, you might change an opinion, but more likely you will simply have a better understanding of why the alternative views make sense to others. (See *p. 40.*)

See the invisible. Select your own object, issue, or topic of study and attach an adjective or descriptive phrase (such as "the First" before "World War") that points out some reality of the situation, ideally some feature that is limiting or taken for granted. Then consider whether your phrase suggests new possibilities or opportunities. This exercise helps you to create interesting and provocative insights. (See *p. 43.*)

 Fire

2. Igniting insights through mistakes: Fail to succeed

- Welcome accidental missteps—let your errors be your guide
- Finding the right question to the wrong answer
- Failing by intent

Fail nine times. The next time you face a daunting challenge, think to yourself, "In order for me to resolve this issue, I will have to fail nine times, but on the tenth attempt, I will be successful." This attitude frees you and allows you to think creatively without fear of failure, because you understand that failure is a forward step toward success. Take a risk and when you fail, no longer think, "Oh, no, what a frustrating waste of time and effort," but instead correctly think, "Great: one down, nine to go—I'm making forward progress!" And indeed you are. After your first failure, think, "Terrific, I'm 10% done!" Mistakes, loss, and failure are all flashing lights clearly pointing the way to deeper understanding and creative solutions. (See *p. 49.*)

Don't stare at a blank screen. Take an issue or problem of interest to you. Just quickly jot down *any* ideas—good, bad, inaccurate, or vague—that you have about the issue. Your ideas will be very bad in many ways. They will be disorganized and jumbled. They will be inaccurate or simply wrong. They'll be impractical. They will be boring. They won't come close to resolving the issue. They won't be creative. Congratulations—excellent start! Now read what you wrote and focus on two features: *what's right* and *what's wrong*. Now you have something to do: tease out the good elements; find particularly nice phrases or pieces of strong ideas; uncover a word that is suggestive of some unstated interesting notion; find that you have clarified for yourself the core of the idea that you want to express. The second task is to recognize and exploit what's wrong and correct the errors you see. You are now doing something different—you are not creating a work on a blank canvas but instead you are responding to a work already there. In making this action item practical, you must be sure to give yourself enough time for the required iterations. (See *p. 59*.)

Have a bad day. Bad days happen to good people. What separates the good from the great is how we react to that bad day. Bad days often include uncomfortably clear lessons about how to grow, learn, or reassess. So the next time you're having a bad day, make the conscious effort to find and extract positive lessons from those not-so-positive experiences. (See *p. 65*.)

Exaggerate to generate errors. Consider an issue or problem and now exaggerate some feature of it to a ridiculous extreme. If you are arguing one side of an issue, support the side you truly believe; then make the argument so exaggerated that you realize that it's way over the top. Now study your exaggerated description and discover some underlying defect. Does that defect also exist in a nonexaggerated perspective? As if you were conducting a stress test, you might apply this exercise to something that works well and learn how it breaks down. The strategy of exaggeration to extremes can be applied to any issue, from writing to marketing to product development to politics. For example, large companies hire hackers to attempt to break into their computer systems to expose security weaknesses. (See *p. 68*.)

 Air

3. Creating questions out of thin air: Be your own Socrates

- How answers can lead to questions
- Creating questions enlivens your curiosity
- What's the *real* question?

Teach to learn. There is no better way to learn anything than to actually teach it, because to teach something you have to confront many fundamental questions: What is the motivation to learn this topic? What are the basic examples? On what aspects of this material should I focus? What are the underlying themes? What ties the ideas together? What is the global structure? What are the important details? These questions force you to discover the heart of the matter and see exactly what you truly understand and what you still need to work on. So consider an idea or topic you are trying to better understand, and ask yourself what you would say if you had to start right now to give a complete explanation, including motivation, examples, overview, and details, of that subject. Better still, prepare a minilecture and then deliver it to someone—family, friends, or even your teacher. (See *p. 79.*)

Improve the question. From a student's point of view, the question "How can I get better grades?" is not the most effective route to higher grades. Questions such as "How can I learn to think better and understand more deeply?" "How can I learn to communicate better?" "How can I increase my curiosity?" are far more constructive. For each question that presents itself in life, craft more focused questions that might lead to a productive conclusion. Try to create questions that expose hidden assumptions, clarify issues, and lead to action. Question your own questions. (See *p. 89.*)

Ask meta-questions. Whether in the classroom, the boardroom, or the living room, asking questions about an assignment or project *before* beginning work in earnest will always lead to a stronger final product. Ask, "What's the goal of this task?" and "What benefit flows from the task?" Keep that benefit in mind as you move forward. A by-product of this exercise is that it often saves time, because it focuses your attention on the core issues and allows you to quickly clear up the initial confusion that always is present at the start of any project or task. (See *p. 91*.)

 Water

4. Seeing the flow of ideas: Look back, look forward

- Understanding current ideas through the flow of ideas
- Creating new ideas from old ones

Iterate ideas. You don't need an army of thousands of individuals to struggle to address a challenge. The only person who needs to move forward little by little is you. Take a homework assignment, essay, or project that you're facing and quickly *just do it*; that is, tackle the questions, draft the essay, or move forward on the project at a fast-forward speed that will surely generate a work that is, at best, subpar. Now consider *that* poor effort as your starting point: react to that work and start to improve and iterate. The flow of iteration will lead to a refined final product. Notice how this flowing mind-set perfectly coincides with the elements of failure we introduced earlier. (See *p. 96*.)

Think back. Whenever you face an issue—whether an area of study or a decision about a future path—consider what came before. Wonder how the issue at hand landed in front of you. Ask where and what it was yesterday, a month ago, a year ago, and so forth. Everything, everyone evolves. Acknowledging that reality as well as considering the subject's history will allow you to generate new insights as well as create fruitful directions in which to move forward. (See *p. 101*.)

Extend ideas. Take a good idea from any arena—work, society, or personal life. It need not be an idea you yourself originated. Now engage with that idea and extend it. The key is not to wonder *whether* the idea has extensions; it does. Your challenge is to find them. (See *p. 108*.)

Once you have it, see if you can improve it. Take a solution to an issue or an essay you've written and create a different, better one. *Assume* there is a mistake or omission or missed opportunity in your work—there always is! Now find it (yet another example of the power of failing). This activity is much more challenging than it might at first appear. We are biased and limited by what we already know—especially since we know it works. However, moving beyond that bias can lead to new answers that, in turn, can lead to new insights and more effective solutions. (See *p. 111*.)

Ask: What were they thinking? What beliefs, cultural habits, opinions, or actions that are completely accepted today will be viewed as ridiculous by our grandchildren? What are some possible candidates? Centuries ago, perfectly respectable people viewed slavery as a natural and moral practice. What practices that we accept as fine today will be condemned as offensive in the future? (See *p. 115*.)

 The Quintessential Element

5. Engaging change: Transform yourself

Expert change. If you're learning something, solving a problem, or developing a skill, imagine in detail what a more skilled practitioner does, or what added knowledge, understanding, and previous experience the expert would bring to the task. In other words, describe the *different* task that an *expert* would be doing compared to what you are currently doing in undertaking your task. Instead of thinking that you are going to be doing something that is harder—requiring more concentration and more effort—think in terms of what kind of knowledge or skill or strategy would make the task an easier one. (See *p. 126*.)

The quintessential you. The first four elements enable you to think better than you do; learn better than you do; and be more creative than you are. The fifth element recommends that you actually do it. *Just do it.* Adopt the habit of improvement, whether using our four elements or by any other methods that you find. If the ability to change is part of who you are, then you are liberated from worry about weaknesses or defects, because you can adapt and improve whenever you like.

Strive for rock-solid understanding (*Earth*).

Fail and learn from those missteps (*Fire*).

Constantly create and ask challenging questions (*Air*).

Consciously consider the flow of ideas (*Water*).

And, of course, remember that learning is a lifelong journey; thus each of us remains a work-in-progress—always evolving, ever changing—and that's *Quintessential* living.

Share Your Own Stories of Effective Thinking

We would love to hear how you apply the elements of effective thinking in your own life. No story is too small or too large. It could be about your personal life or your work life. It could be about a small issue or an experience that transformed you or an entire organization. In addition, feel free to send us stories that are not your own, but instead are instances in which the elements of effective thinking have changed other individuals or institutions—maybe even changed the course of history.

We seek actual examples of real-life applications of these elements of thinking. If the story is not from your own experience, then also include the source in which you found it—perhaps a book, newspaper, or website.

Please visit www.elementsofthinking.com to share with us an application of the elements of effective thinking. Thank you for helping to spread effective thinking.

Acknowledgments

One theme of this book is that ideas arise from many sources, and certainly many sources were important in the creation of this book. Here we would like to thank a few of the many people who directly or inadvertently helped us to conceptualize this work. In some sense, our entire careers and personal experiences have influenced this book's creation. First we would like to thank all the students, faculty members, business leaders, professionals, lifelong learners, and friends and family members who gave us the decades of foundational experiences from which this work emerged. We thank them all for inspiring us to distill the fundamentals of innovation, learning, and creativity down to five elements. We are particularly grateful to all those who read early manuscript versions and offered important perspectives, suggestions, and criticisms that allowed us to improve the book. Beyond the many students who offered suggestions, we wish to acknowledge the contributions of Martha Bradshaw, Jack Canfield, Caryn Carlson, John Chandler, Charles Davis, Elizabeth Davis, Betty Sue Flowers, Brad Henry, Scott Hillstrom, Ron Kidd, Paul King, Tony Plog, Kristen Pond, Cesar Silva, Will Stanton, Greg Starbird, Paul Stueck, Phil Styrlund, and Fay Vincent.

Finally, we wish to thank the entire staff at Princeton University Press for their energy, creativity, and vision in making this book a reality. We especially wish to thank Vickie Kearn, executive editor, for her personal support, enthusiasm, and hard work. We thank Peter Dougherty, director of the Press, who immediately appreciated and supported the goals of this project. We thank Quinn Fusting, editorial assistant; Lauren Lepow, senior editor; Jessica Pellien, assistant publicity director; Caroline Priday, European director of publicity; and Karl Spurzem, designer, who have used and are using their talents and expertise both to produce a beautiful book and to allow it to reach its full potential audience. We greatly appreciate everyone at Princeton University Press for making this continuing collaboration an enjoyable adventure.

Edward Burger: I wish to thank Elizabeth Davis, executive vice president and provost at Baylor University, for providing me with the opportunity to put some of the themes of this book into practice at an institutional level, and for her support, inspiration, and friendship. I also wish to acknowledge my loving parents, Florence and Sandor Burger, who were the first to teach me the transformational potential of thinking and creativity. Finally, it is a great pleasure to thank my collaborator, Mike Starbird—whose wisdom, insights, encouragement, and friendship over the past twenty years have truly enriched my life.

Michael Starbird: I would like to give special thanks to my friends and family members who have been so supportive and encouraging in all ways. My wife, Roberta Starbird, and our daughters, Talley and Bryn, helped me not only by offering specific ideas regarding this book but more importantly by creating a foundational and loving environment for joyful living. The most enjoyable and inspirational part of this project has been and continues to be the pleasure of working with my friend and collaborator, Ed Burger. Ed is a fount of creative ideas and boundless energy, which it has been my privilege and pleasure to delight in for many years.

Edward Burger

Edward Burger is president of Southwestern University and an educational and business consultant. Formerly, he was the Francis Christopher Oakley Professor of Mathematics at Williams College and served as a vice provost at Baylor University. He has authored or coauthored over 65 articles, books, and video series; delivered over 500 addresses and workshops throughout the world; and made over 50 radio and television appearances—at broadcasting venues including ABC, NBC, Discovery, and NPR. Burger has received over 25 awards and honors for his teaching and scholarly work. In particular, he received the 2001 Mathematical Association of America Deborah and Franklin Tepper Haimo National Award for Distinguished Teaching of Mathematics, was named the 2001–2003 Polya Lecturer, was awarded the Chauvenet Prize in 2004 and the Lester R. Ford Prize in 2006, and won four awards for his video work, including two Telly Awards in 2010 and 2013. In 2007 Williams College awarded him the Nelson Bushnell Prize for Scholarship and Teaching. In 2006, *Reader's Digest* listed Burger in their annual

"100 Best of America" as America's Best Math Teacher. In 2010 he was named the winner of the Robert Foster Cherry Award for Great Teaching—the largest and most prestigious prize in higher education teaching across all disciplines in the English-speaking world. Also in 2010 he starred in a mathematics segment for NBC-TV on the *Today* show and throughout the 2010 Winter Olympic coverage. The *Huffington Post* named him one of their 2010 Game Changers; "HuffPost's Game Changers salutes 100 innovators, visionaries, mavericks, and leaders who are reshaping their fields and changing the world."

Michael Starbird

Michael Starbird is University Distinguished Teaching Professor of Mathematics at The University of Texas at Austin. He has been a visiting scholar at the Institute for Advanced Study in Princeton, New Jersey, and a member of the technical staff at the Jet Propulsion Laboratory in Pasadena, California. He has received fifteen significant teaching awards, including the 2001 Mathematical Association of America Deborah and Franklin Tepper Haimo National Award for Distinguished Teaching of Mathematics, the Texas-wide Minnie Stevens Piper Professorship, an inaugural year UT Regents Outstanding Teaching Award and nearly every university-wide teaching award The

University of Texas offers—including, among others, the Jean Holloway Award, the Friar Society Centennial Teaching Fellowship, and the President's Associates Teaching Excellence Award. He is a member of UT's Academy of Distinguished Teachers. Starbird has delivered hundreds of addresses at colleges, universities, and conferences around the country and has conducted dozens of workshops, especially aimed to help teach effective thinking. He has produced DVD courses in the Great Courses series on calculus, statistics, probability, geometry, and the joy of thinking, which introduce hundreds of thousands of people to the pleasures of ideas. His other books with coauthor Edward Burger include the award-winning textbook *The Heart of Mathematics: An Invitation to Effective Thinking* and the general-audience book *Coincidences, Chaos, and All That Math Jazz: Making Light of Weighty Ideas*. With Edward Odell and David Marshall, he coauthored the textbook *Number Theory through Inquiry*. With Brian Katz, he coauthored the textbook *Distilling Ideas: An Introduction to Mathematics through Inquiry*. His success at teaching people to think has been recognized by more than fifteen awards, including the highest national teaching award in his field as well as statewide and university-wide honors selected from all disciplines.